CW01617453

Landlor
in New Ze

Landlording in New Zealand

A complete manual for rental property owners

Second Edition

Frank Saxton Mgt. Dip.

Published by F.L. Saxton & Associates
P O Box 790
NELSON

Dedicated to my father Leighton. I loved you.

Acknowledgments

Thanks to my friend Alan Harding and my sister Anne for helping me with the text. Also, thanks to all the anonymous tenants who provide stories that run through the text.

This book is sold subject to the understanding that the author and publisher are not engaged in rendering legal or accounting advice or service. If legal or other expert advice outside the scope of this book is sought the services of a competent professional person should be obtained.

Laws governing property ownership, rental and investment and other issues related to this book are subject to change. The author and publisher accept no responsibility whatsoever for any consequences arising from the use of any information in this book. or the forms provided with it.

First published 1994 by
F.L. Saxton & Associates
417 Wakefield Quay
NELSON
New Zealand

Reprinted 1995
Second edition 1996
Reprinted 1997, 1998, 2000

Copyright © 1994 F.L. Saxton

This book is copyright. Except for the purpose of fair review, no part may be stored or transmitted in any form or by any means, electronic or mechanical, including recording or storage in any information retrieval system, without permission in writing from the publisher. No reproduction may be made, by photocopying or by any other means, unless a licence has been obtained from the publisher or its agent. However, the forms provided with this book may freely be photocopied and used by the original purchaser.

ISBN 0-473-02712-7

Illustrations and cover design by Errol McLeary
Typeset in Times Roman and designed by Orca Publishing Services, Christchurch
Edited by .303 Associates

Printed by PrintLink

Contents

Author's note

Throughout this book the notation "s." means section of the Residential Tenancies Act, as for example s.17(1)(a) refers to the Residential Tenancies Act 1986 Section 17 subsection (1) paragraph (a). In the Act the term "landlord" refers to both males and females who undertake the role of managing residential rental property. This is an old-fashioned, gender-exclusive term, and we need a new sexually inclusive word — do you know one? I don't. I don't invent one here; I just take the easy way out and use the terminology of parliament where, irrespective of sex, we are all called by the male term — landlords.

Note to the second edition

In these changing times extensive revisions have become necessary since this book was first published in 1994 and reprinted in 1995. The most important and extensive of these concern the Residential Tenancies Act (Ch. 5). The forms which were originally provided separately have also been added as appendices. These may be freely photocopied for use by the original purchaser of the book.

Introduction

I bought my first flats in the early 1980s whilst working as a public servant. After being made redundant in 1988, I worked with a real estate firm as rental-property manager. This gave me experience in renting all types of residential property, from up-market executive houses to low-cost blocks of flats. Nowadays my residential-rental work is concentrated on those properties I own. Recently I purchased a block of suburban shops as a first venture into commercial property.

When I bought my first flats in 1984 it seemed logical to join the landlords' "club", which in my home town of Nelson is called the Nelson Property Investors Association. As in most small non-profit organisations anyone who shows interest is likely to be shanghaied on to the committee and I soon began a number of years in the positions of secretary and president. In doing so I mixed with other landlords and property professionals, acquiring much factual information but perhaps more importantly also learning the ethics, beliefs, and attitudes of property people.

In 1991 and 1992, a fellow club member and city father, Seddon Marshall, and I produced a series of introductory rental-property investment courses in Nelson. In the process of writing this book I have tried to answer many of the usual questions asked by students on these courses.

About the residential-rental industry

When I bought my first rental property, inflation was entrenched and seemed here to stay. Interest rates were creeping up, then along with wages and prices they became fixed by law only to become free again and rise alarmingly. There was much public enthusiasm about the profits of the share market. Commercial property was seen as both an exciting and secure way of generating wealth; residential rental was the poor relation. Nowadays, things are probably the reverse of that.

The watershed between now and then is October 1987 when the sharemarket leapt over the cliff. Commercial property values soon followed and gently lowered themselves down the cliff-face. Throughout both periods of climbing and falling, however, residential-rental generally kept on as a steady business. Even as unemployment increased and many people no longer went to the now-vacant office and industrial sites to work, they still came home at night to sleep. Perhaps because of this history of stability among the storms, the residential rental industry has of late had the spotlight turned on it. At times it even seems to be presented as a glamour investment. However, this is only the "front door" view. From the back door, as it were, the scene is one of work. The tasks of planning, managing and controlling sit about the backyard needing attention. From this view it is a business competing with perhaps a second job, or the alternative to joining the work force — perhaps for the caregiver in a partnership.

About this book

This book acknowledges the crucial role of the investment motive in property ownership and discusses the most common theories of property investment analysis. Most emphasis, however, is on the practical aspects of running a business where financial skills, people skills, handyperson skills, knowledge of the law, and other skills are all part of the repertoire of the successful operator.

I write primarily for the do-it-yourself residential landlord — or those who wish to become so. Chapter 1 covers both the process of tax planning before purchase and the investment-making process of buying. Chapter 2 covers many of the more important areas of decision-making you will be involved in. Next is a short chapter examining such items such as the telephone, bank accounts, and personal computer. Next are two substantial chapters, one selecting tenants and the other examining in detail the Residential Tenancies Act 1986. Three shorter chapters follow, on rent collection, record keeping, and maintenance of the rental house and its fittings.

Why go into rental property investment?

The reason for being a landlord is to acquire the income stream generated from the rents. The reason tenants pay rents is to acquire somewhere to live. A roof over one's head is a basic human need. Thus we have a marketplace where buyers and sellers meet. But why *become* a seller of rental accommodation? There is some debate about the wisdom of this.

Arguments for the business

1. It is an easy entry point for first-time property investors. People who already own their own house can buy something similar and already know how to look after it.
2. Like pawnbrokers, who take goods of value in exchange for cash, when you borrow money from a bank you usually need something of value to offer as security. If you offer residential housing you are able to borrow more money in relation to its value than any other asset.
3. It is a big market. Towns that measure their commercial premises in the hundreds measure their residential rentals in the thousands. The advantage of big markets is that they are usually stable and easy to get in and out of.
4. Many rental properties can also be sold to homeowners. This gives a measure of security if tenant demand declines.
5. The mean-spirited tax of stamp duty does not apply to residential property (whereas it does to commercial property). Also, residential investment property has a better depreciation rate for tax purposes than the average depreciation experienced (although beware: you have to pay it back when you sell).
6. A small number of rentals can easily be run as a small business alongside other work.
7. Capital gain is likely to accrue over the long term as a function of the rising costs of building any new competing housing stock.
8. In the 1916 New Zealand census, 53% of all householders in New Zealand owned the house they lived in. In the 1991 census it was 76%. This growth occurred, I believe, because of government support for home ownership. The taxpayer (or offshore lender!) funded such government schemes as the capitalisation of the family benefit, below market interest rates and higher than market loan-to-deposit ratios. A government department became a multi-billion-dollar bank to home owners. Now, government housing support tied to home ownership has disappeared. It thus seems likely that New Zealand's rate of homeownership will fall to something nearer 50% which is typical of O.E.C.D. countries. This means that by buying into residential-rental you are buying into a growing industry.
9. The generation of New Zealanders currently on taxpayer-funded retirement incomes have enjoyed middle-class lifestyles of a quality that their parents never had nor their children can expect. Providing for

one's own retirement is now a recognised goal and residential-rental property provides a basis for a "do-it-yourself" superannuation fund.

Arguments against the business

1. New Zealand has too much capital in its housing stock — in particular, middle-class home-owning suburbs full of houses with empty bedrooms. As households begin to be forced to secure a cash flow for retirement from their capital resource there will be a drift of value from residential property to revenue-earning investment. This is likely to result in the capital gain of residential property over the next 20 years being less than inflation.
2. To achieve social goals, governments are often tempted to intervene in rental-housing markets. Such intervention is usually at the expense of the landlord and introduces uncertainty.
3. If you have too many angry nights of sleeplessness fuming over delinquent tenant behaviour, this business may not be for you. Education and experience help enormously, but we all have our own strengths and weaknesses and tenant management may be not good for your stress levels. Likewise, the risks of borrowing mortgage money may produce anxiety beyond your level of tolerance.

There is much factual information in this book — fuel for the logical process. But besides ones head there is also ones heart. What are some of the feelings, and the untested beliefs, as it were, of landlords?

The buying property "mood".

In this world there are people who are over-the-top optimistic and think nothing can ever go wrong with their schemes. In quick succession they make and attempt ever more fantastic ones. They might be called manic people. At the other extreme are very depressed people who believe everything they do will turn out bad. They adopt a mood of ill-humour, withdraw into themselves, play safe and do nothing out there in the dangerous big world.

My question is, what is it to be "normal"? Is it to be half-way between these two extremes? I suppose if a computer were asked to work it out it might agree that half-way is where the "real world" is. However, I believe the computer would be wrong. It seems to me "normal" people — well, at least the average normal property investor (if you will allow me to call us normal!) — is slightly on the manic side of half-way.

You see, to buy property is to take a leap into the dark. It involves big amounts of money, most of it usually borrowed, and if things go wrong it is a quick way to go broke. To buy property this way is not entirely logical. At least, I vividly recall one property I bought when I wasn't thinking that straight.

My marriage had just broken up. We owned our house and a year before had bought another one that was divided up into two flats, we rented the flats out. I suddenly found out with horror, when the matrimonial split-up took its toll, that I only owned one.

I just wanted to get back to owning two properties. This old house, in a good area, was for sale for $55,000 and I bought if for $47,000 (the date was 1986). I financed it by raising a first mortgage against it and increasing the mortgage on the place I owned, I didn't use any of my own money (I had none anyway). The land agent I bought it through was very supportive of my decision.

It was during the weekend afterwards, when having a good look over it, I began to realise how bad it was. The following Monday I saw the place still advertised in the window of another real-estate agency. I went in and asked about it — even though I had already bought it — to get another opinion, I suppose. A young salesman served me, "That one? Its a redevelopment job — bulldozer material, land value only", he said dismissively. I guess he knew I wasn't a property developer — he was right about that. So I was stuck with a crook building.

The piles would be an archaeologist's delight. While most of them were totara ones that had unfortunately rotted before they got a chance to fossilise, others were short lengths of some ancient form of masonry sewer pipe stood on their ends. The exterior was stucco over weather-boards. Mostly rotten boards, I suppose

The roof was really bad. I would say it was the worst house-roof in town. I sort of became a bit of an expert on roofs — looking up at them, hoping to find one similar. The corrugated iron was rusted badly all over, often rusted through where one sheet of iron overlapped the one below. Short lengths of corrugated iron had been slipped under, thatching style. Even some of these patches were themselves now rusting through. With the words "bulldozer material" running through my head, I wasn't going to spend money putting a new roof on. I wire-brushed the rusty iron, cut new patches and put them under the laps. I put rust-kill on and primed the whole lot before applying a couple of top coats. (Actually, at the time I was angry with my ex-wife and I sort of took it out on the roof!)

At least once a year since, I have had to trace new leaks and occasionally patch again. I have never bothered to re-paint. The years go by.

The flooring is another story. Years ago a neighbour had used his side of my house as a retaining wall. About a metre of soil was piled up against the stucco exterior, and floor boards have rotted all along that side. One tactic (when a tenant falls through and complains) was to pull up the rotten boards and if it is not far down to the ground, mix up concrete in a barrow outside, wheel it in and fill the hole. Floor-coverings cover all. I dug all the soil away from that side of the house to uncover the air vents and dry out underneath.

The saving graces of the old wreck is that it is in a good area, it gets loads of sun, is close to town and has generous-sized rooms. Depending on how you classify the rooms, both flats are either one or two bedrooms each. And they rent well. The building has got 'character' in a town where few flats have. I painted and re-carpeted (second-hand commercial grade) inside; the flats have a homely feel.

It has a great cash-flow. Despite the heavy borrowing, it nearly broke even on the tax form in the first year. Since then it has pleased the IRD with the useful taxable profits it has made. The Government valuation has gone up and the current one (October 1991) is $76,000. I don't know who would buy it though. Probably a re-developer — although these days there is a shortage of character "doer-uppers" and some energetic young couple might make it their restoration masterpiece. Here's hoping, anyway!

Maybe I have overstated my case with this rather extreme example, but nevertheless I believe one needs a chunk of the old incorrigible optimist aboard — even the merest hint of mania at times, perhaps — to make those buying decisions. These are the decisions that get one into the property business. Actually, being a landlord can be like being in the military — intense periods of activity followed by long periods of boredom for the survivors. However, even in these long periods there is the week-to-week management of tenants.

Landlord use-by date.

When I joining the local Property Investors Association, I met other landlords. I generalise here of course, but it seemed to me they were optimistic when they bought their rentals. They did so in order to do deals, own property and make money. Somewhere in the back of their minds (I'm no exception) I reckon is a hidden Bob Jones lurking about. On the other hand, most people who I saw give up the business seemed to be doing so because they wanted to be rid of the job of managing domestic tenants. Not, you'll note, because they were failing to make money (even if it was not on the Bob Jones scale).

From this observation I figured the life of being a residential landlord may be a limited thing. Maybe there is something that gets used up and worn out. I don't know that this thing is called — some might call it goodwill to mankind perhaps, or good humour. Whatever it is, the trick must be to make it last as long as possible — so one can make the most money! And also, I guess, if it matters to you, to have a happy life at the same time! It must come down to being able to handle difficult tenants without too much stress on oneself, I figure.

Controlling tenants may be compared with controlling cars, perhaps. My first car was one of those tall telephone-box-shaped ones, a 1952 Ford Prefect. When it came to a corner, my dealings with all the levers and the wheel in front of the driver's seat had to be done just right — it could never be taken for granted. It preferred to know about the corner long before we got there, proper road speed applied — but never braking and cornering at the same time, and also no changing gears on corners. Also, it liked to be kept near the middle of the road where it is flatter. To drive it I had to get on side with it. One day we didn't agree and it fell over on a corner with me still in it. We both acquired minor damage.

Nowadays I drive one of those wide low cars the shape of an upside-down dinner plate (a Honda Prelude). I sit, it seems, only about six inches above the ground. There is no body roll, it has quick-response power steering and wide flat tyres that stick to the road like chewing gum. If I tell it to go around a corner, it goes no matter what. There is no doubt as to who is in control.

When I started landlording, I thought all I needed to do was to be nice to my tenants and they would be nice back. When the exceptions came, and they weren't nice back, I was rather lost. I would end up saying things like, "I am very disappointed in you Simon, you promised when you moved in to do x and y. Now you have done z on me. I thought we were going to be friends but now I feel I can't trust you." Also, I would write letters with phrases such as: "It is stipulated in the agreement that..." and

"I insist you do immediately x ..."

Behind my "nice" theory was really a belief about control. Control and obedience was expected in return for my "niceness". (Perhaps I have transferred my need for control to the way I drive my car!)

Nowadays, being "nice" isn't one of my objectives. What I aim to be is what my father would call being "straight up and down". I aim to clearly state my position and then allow the tenants to choose theirs in relation to mine. In this process we both become responsible for the outcome of our own choosing.

There is more of a personal detachment in me I guess. For example, I have a budget that doesn't demand I collect rent every 52 weeks of the year. I am friendly towards my tenants and I guess I smile a lot. I am interested in understanding them as individuals. However, I have no need to be their friend.

I run my business more by running the system that runs my business than by controlling it directly. I run it the way I used to drive my old Prefect car — with plenty of forward planning and getting all the levers and the wheel in their proper order before the corners. We still might leave the road from time to time, mind you, but at least it won't be all my fault; the tenant will have to take some of the blame for their part in the choices they made as well.

I guess this is what some writers call having the "correct attitude" to landlording. Actually, "attitude" is the angle an aeroplane chooses to take in relation to the horizontal. Sometimes their attitude gets them flying and at other times they crash. Anyway, all I can say, is that my "use-by" date hasn't come up yet, I hope I've still got a little humour and goodwill in reserve.

Chapter 1

Buying and tax planning

Begin tax planning before you buy. I cannot stress this too strongly. My accountant tells me that at tax time clients come to him who have bought rental property in the last year. On examining their affairs, he discovers they have purchased their property the wrong way. This typically means they now have to pay hundreds or even thousands of dollars of tax that they would not be liable to pay if they had done it another way — the right way.

In this section on tax planning I will give examples of tax problems in a story-like manner. I want you to be alerted to the problems of tax law, but without bothering you with all the details. Such a detailed description is beyond the scope of this book. Indeed it is beyond the scope of any book, because tax law is constantly changing, both by revision of statutes and as key cases come before the courts. To be up-to-date, you need to be practicing tax law. As an investor, I buy this up-to-date knowledge from those professionals (accountants and lawyers) who are practicing.

There are two important issues to discuss here: firstly the question of tax deductibility of interest and secondly the problem of "tainting".

Tax deductibility of interest

When buying a property, most landlords borrow some or all of the purchase price. In doing so they buy into a liability as well as an asset. Planning for this liability needs to start before you acquire it.

Once, when I was young and innocent, I shifted from one flat (where I had heaps of equity) to another (where I had heaps of debt). I shifted so I could paint the other flat in in my spare time. However, at tax time, I found

I had more than $2,000 in extra tax to pay for the year. This was because the interest on the loan raised to buy the flat I now lived in was now no longer tax deductable, while the flat I had moved from was making large taxable profits. If I had stayed put and not shifted, it would have been cheaper to hire a gang of painters to do the paint job! I shifted back to the first flat as quickly as I could to stop this cash haemorrhage to the I.R.D.

When raising a loan, as much attention needs to be given to how the loan is raised as to the interest rate and fees charged for it. You want your loan to be eligible for tax deductions.

Currently there is a slogan the Inland Revenue Department are using: "It's our job to be fair". This is rubbish. They can *never* be fair because taxation itself is not based on fairness: it is simply an opportunist activity of governments. They get their money wherever they can. Some people pay huge amounts of tax in their lifetime while others only ever take from the public purse. What's fair about that?

In the words of Judge D.J. Barber: "...there is no fairness in tax other than entitlement to a fair hearing and a proper application of the law. Either the transaction procedure provides deductibility [of mortgage interest] or it does not. It does not help that another procedure could have achieved deductility..."

This quote comes from a Taxation Review Authority Case (TRA 88/171; Dec. No 58/91). In this case the taxpayer, a schoolteacher, bought a flat, in a block of two, with her savings. She lived in it without a mortgage and in due course retired. A few years later the neighbouring flat came on the market, she bought it and shifted into it (it was more sunny). She borrowed most of the money to make this second purchase by taking out a mortgage on her first flat, rather than selling it. She did it this way in order to make some long-term provisions for retirement income, and rented out her old flat. The I.R.D. required that she pay a lot of tax from her rent money. However, she no longer had the rent money because she had spent it on paying her mortgage interest. The judge found the I.R.D. was correct. As he pointed out, it made no difference that with some professional advice she could have done the paperwork differently at the time of purchase and achieved a much lower tax bill.

The key to the deductibility of mortgage interest is *the purpose for which the mortgage was taken out.* For example, I met a friend of mine who is in the process of transferring to Dunedin because of his job. He owned a mortgage-free house that was up for sale. He said, "I have just been thinking that instead of simply buying a nice house in Dunedin to live in, I could split my capital three ways and buy three houses down there. I'd have a mortgage on each and rent two of them out, and just like you've been doing, build up some investment income."

The first thing I said was, "Get some professional tax advice before you buy".

"Why, what would the advice be? I've never been to an accountant in my life," he said.

"I don't know," I said. "I'm not a tax expert, but to give you some idea the advice may be first of all to buy, without a mortgage, the house you want to live in. Live in it and then raise a mortgage against it to get your deposit-capital back to buy the other two. Doing it this way all the mortgages are raised for the purpose of acquiring the rental units — and so *all* the interest is deductable against the rents.

"I say this because the way you just said it to me before — 'I would split the money into three' — I imagined you doing just that and buying your own house with a mortgage from day one, using only a third of your money, leaving the other two-thirds in the bank. The problem is that as long as you live in that house the interest on the mortgage on it must be paid out of your own tax-paid income — at least the way I figure it."

He still looked a bit confused. I said, "I usually find it difficult to explain to the uninitiated property investor. It seems to be somehow simple in theory but complicated in practice. That is why I say, ask around down in Dunedin and by word of mouth select a good accountant and get advice before you buy. All individual finances and situations are as unique as personalities, and must be analysed on a case-by-case basis."

Tainting

One of the taxation diseases to avoid is tainting. This is the alarming capacity of one business activity to have the effect of creating a taxation liability in another. For example, being a landlord means the reason you own property is to collect rent — this is your business. If you sell your property in the future for more than you paid for it, the capital gain you made is not taxable, as you are simply dealing with your capital and not the "product" of the business. On the other hand, if you are a builder, developer or trader of property, then the property transactions themselves are the vehicle for producing the revenue and hence the profit of the business. Any rent these businesses may collect is secondary to their main activity.

The practical effect of this distinction is that for the best management of your taxation as a landlord, you need to keep all your landlording-property transactions safe from being regarded as the other kind.

Take the example of Joe Bloggs, who owns a couple of investment rental properties and then purchases a third block of flats at a mortgagee sale. He buys them because they are run down and going cheap. He fixes them up, puts them on separate titles and sell them off for a profit over a period of 12 to 18 months. This makes him a developer and trader, and as such he expects to pay tax on the entire profits of the exercise. However, perhaps in that same tax year he also sells a flat he has owned for 4 years and has been renting out as a regular landlord. He is now likely to be assessed as a trader on this property as well and have its "capital gain" taxed. What is happening here is all his property dealings are beginning to be tainted by the trader activity.

The main weapon in the fight against tainting is separate ownership structures. If that block of run-down flats is bought by a company set up expressly for that purpose, then what the company does in its name is kept separate from what Joe does in his own name. It is safe from tainting. Once again, professional advice *before* purchase is the key.

Investment decision making: deciding what is a good buy

When it comes to buying a rental property, there are many different types. There are blocks of flats lying in the sun like long sausages. Alongside may be tidy ownership units smelling of grandmothers and flower gardens, advertised as suitable for "investment". Down the road may be old houses divided up into student flats with posters on the walls. Across town there may be even older, dilapidated houses on industrial land with empty beer bottles out the back. Away in other areas are three-bedroom suburban houses lined up in neat rows.

Even when you do decide to buy into one particular rental type the diversity only diminishes; it never disappears altogether. Real estate is a collection of unique individuals. If you buy a property there is not another identical one to compare it with. Even in a row of flats all built the same and for sale on separate titles, there are differences. One will be on the end that gets most of the sun — or most of the shade, or more traffic — or the one in the middle will get noise from both sides, or the one next to it is shaded by the neighbour's tree. This is different from shares: a parcel of one thousand Fletcher Challenge shares is identical to any other one thousand parcel of Fletcher Challenger shares. The difference is important to the investor.

I remember looking at an old house divided up into 3 flats. I compared it with other rental property, and it was an OK buy but didn't stand out as anything special. My friend bought it. Within a few months he was approached by a buyer who offered 50% more than he'd paid for it, conditional on gaining a zoning exemption from the council. The zoning was granted and the building was removed, and a service station was built on the site. Nothing was seen at the time of the original purchase to suggest this property was any different to the other rentals for sale.

Whenever I buy a property I am aware that I am the only one doing so. It is a lonely feeling. Why me? Am I doing the right thing here?

The uniqueness of each property underlies why marketing them is unpredictable. A well priced property may languish on the market without a buyer, or the converse may apply when a high-priced property sells in the first few days after it enters the market. The vendor of each property has a kind of monopoly: no other property is quite the same as theirs and whether there is a buyer for it at the time it is placed on the market, is something of a gamble.

This unique situation has caused two institutions to sprung up:

Real Estate Agents. These professionals offer a service as brokers for the property market. The figure varies from town to town and from time to time but from what I can gather about 70-80% of all properties that change hands do so with the involvement of an agent (the rest are private sales). Of the 8 properties I have bought, 6 of them I obtained through agents (in fact 5 of them through the one agency which trades in the Harcourts group). A personal relationship with an agent over some 15 years now has been the way I have accessed the market. At the end of the day, the best way to buy a property is from a seller who is keen to sell, and people anxious to sell typically do so through agents.

As a novice buyer, I found that I have been able to gain a view of the market through the eyes of an estate agent as he has showed me what is for sale and what has recently sold. Agents, through their knowledge and listings, make it easier to "comparison buy". This is the simple process whereby value is assessed by comparing one property to another. In New Zealand, the seller almost always pays the agent so in law they are the seller's agent and have to act in the seller's interest. In practice agents act more as a mediator and bring the two parties together into a contract.

Valuers. These professionals will assess the market value of any property. Their reports are relied upon by lenders as a basis for judging how much money to advance against the security of the property. The task of a valuer and that of the investor are similar. We are both in the business of measuring worth.

There are a number of different methods used for assessing the value of income-producing property. Let us now look at some of these. In discussing the various methods we will use an example of a block of four flats. You don't have to understand all the financial details of these flats yet, I intend to use this as we read on and I will refer back to the data of this example.

An example:

	$ capital	$ per year
Purchase price (4 flats)		250,000
Equity (or deposit)	100,000	
Mortgage at 10% interest only	150,000	-15,000 (interest)
Gross rental income (4 flats at $135 each, 52 weeks year)		28,080
Building's depreciation ($200,000 at 3% per year)		- 6,000
Rates		- 1,600
Insurance		- 450
Maintenance (5% of gross rents)		- 1,400
Vacancies (2 weeks each unit)		- 1,080
Sale price at end of 10 years	335,000	
Net return on sale	235,000	=======
Gross taxable income		2,550
Add back depreciation		6,000
TOTAL BEFORE-TAX INCOME		8,550
TOTAL AFTER-TAX INCOME		7,683

(Allowance for management @ 7% of rents collected - 1,890)

Rate of return valuation method

This is the most common method used by both investors and valuers when looking at rental properties. The fundamental reason for being a landlord is to collect the rent. The flow of rent, week by week, is like a small stream in the desert flowing out of a spring. We want to be the owner of that spring. The value of the spring is measured by the quantity of the water that comes out of it. With no water, it is just another dent in the desert — and dents come pretty cheaply. So it is with rental property. Rental property value can be measured by the quantity and reliability of the rent flow and this is what the rate of return method does.

It was one of the Greek philosophers who first identified the rate of return theory. He said the value of corn determines the value of land — it's not the other way around. You cannot spend a lot of money on an expensive property, add up your annual costs, divide by 52 and say that is the rent. The rent might be too high and the property remain vacant.

Gross rate of return

If you put $250,000 in the bank and earn $25,000 interest, that works out at 10%. In our example the value of the four flats is $250,000 and the gross annual rent is $28,080. By dividing the rent by the purchase price we get 0.112 (or 11.2%). This is the gross rate of return for the four flats. (This is also called the capitalisation rate — cap rate for short.)

How gross rates of return are used

When properties are sold, valuers, real estate agents and active property investors are all keen to know the sale price. Whenever I hear a recent sale price, I can quickly calculate a gross rate of return from knowing the market rent levels in my town. In calculating the rate, I am looking to detect any trend in it, because it changes over time and as an investor I am interested in knowing about any such change, up or down.

For example, I bought a block of flats in 1987 for $160,000, when the rents added up to $640 a week. This gave a gross rate of return of 20.8%. In 1993 the rents were $635 a week, because rents had stayed practically the same in my town for 5 years. A couple of months ago, however, a similar block of flats sold for $268,000. The market rents of that block add up to $590 per week — a gross rate of return of 11.4%. From this I can estimate the present market value of my flats. I calculate this by working the above rate of return calculation in reverse, thus: The annual rent is \$635 x 52 = \$33,020, which I then divide by the rate of return for the comparable flats recently sold (0.114, which is the same as 11.4%). This gives a new market value of \$290,000, which represents a capital increase in value of \$130,000 over and above my purchase price of \$160,000 5 years ago.

When I bought these flats in 1987 I got a first mortgage at 20% and thought this was a great deal because I wasn't paying 22% which was what I had budgeted on. Now I am paying 7.4%. My experience has been one of stable rent levels, falling interest rates and a falling rate of return. As it has become cheaper to borrow money it has also become more profitable to buy rental property with borrowed money — and more people have wanted to do so, thereby forcing up the price of properties for sale.

However, there isn't necessarily any cause-and-effect relationship between interest rates and capital value. The bottom line is that there is a supply of rental properties for sale and a demand for them. The relative strength of these two competing forces determines the price. Like all markets, it seems, the residential rental market contains emotion and reason in about equal proportions.

For example, when in 1986 the Residential Tenancies Act was introduced it rattled many existing landlords and scared off others who might have been thinking of entering the business. It was a great time to be a buyer because there weren't many others. Come 1993, in my town at least, there was a strong demand from people wanting to get in to the business, and it has been like this for a couple of years now. They had seen the sharemarket crash, the decline of commercial property investment, and interest rates had come down on bank deposits — even the price of gold had gone nowhere for years. Residential rental seemed to be the last bolthole of wealth, and sentiment was in full flood. Meanwhile, the Act had not yet been amended even once. It is easy to get caught up in the sentiment of the moment and forget the fundamentals.

When using rates of return you have to be careful to compare like with like. It is not appropriate to compare all rental properties with one another using the same rate of return. New permanent-material blocks of flats, for example, will have a lower rate than older wooden-clad blocks of flats. This natural difference is known as the spread of rates. In a property-boom, this spread often narrows as the cheaper, poorer-quality properties increase in price faster than the better quality ones increase. With the coming of a more settled market, the spread can be expected to widen again as the prices of the poorer-quality fall faster than do the prices for the better quality ones.

Net rate of return

This method is a refinement of the gross rate. It differs from the gross rate of return in the way it deducts from the rents the fixed cash-flow expenses of the property. These expenses are the rates, insurance, maintenance, management and vacancy factor. In our example (see p.20) these expenses total $6,420. This does not include depreciation, because it is an expense you do not have to front up with cash for. Nor are the interest costs of the mortgage deducted. The reason the interest costs are not deducted is because they vary, depending on who owns the property. This method thus enables you to compare objectively one property with another — irrespective of who owns which. In our example, the expenses of $6,420 are deducted from the gross rent of $28,080 to get a net rent of $21,660. When this is divided into the purchase price of $250,000 we get 0.086 (8.6%), which is the net rate of return.

There are differences in the way different people calculate net rents. For example how much are we to deduct for the maintenance expenses? In this example I have used 5% of rents. This figure feels right to me given my experience with long-term ownership of flats. It will vary between different types of property: weatherboard buildings require more money for maintenance than stucco ones for example. Another controversial expense is the 7% management fee. Most owners manage their own properties and never incur this cost. The reason I include it is because this is something close to what it is likely to cost a professional manager to manage a block of flats. By calculating the net return this way I find I can make valid comparisons with other forms of investment. For example, I can make a direct comparison between residential and commercial property investment. In the commercial formula I use a 3% figure for management because commercial tenants require less management effort.

For this method to work, it is not particularly important what formula you use to arrive at your net expenses. What is vital is that the same method be used on each property. Different valuers may use differing formulae. If you are given a net rate of return for a particular property you need to check how the deductable expenses were arrived at.

How net rates of return are used

Net rates are typically used when a more careful and detailed evaluation of property is called for. For example, when buying further property I calculate the net rate for each property offered to me. I don't trust the gross rate when it comes to making important decisions.

Gearing ratios

Other names for this are asset/liability ratio and debt/equity ratio. They are a simple measure of what you own compared to what you owe. In our example the block of four flats is worth $250,000 and has a mortgage of $150,000. This a debt/equity ratio of 60%, and an asset/liability ratio of 1.6 to 1. These ratios are measurements of risk — the risk being that if things go wrong, you have to pay the bank back first before there is any money left for you.

Usually, banks will lend on first mortgage a higher percentage of a residential property's total value than they will against any other form of security. This gives the residential-rental investor a greater choice of the level of borrowing to operate at. In the capitalist system there is no free lunch. For every benefit there is a corresponding cost. The benefit of borrowed money is being able to operate a bigger business. Indeed, you are likely to need borrowed money to operate at all. Bigger businesses generally mean bigger profits. Borrowing money, however, also means the taking on-board of an increased risk. If things go wrong and you make a loss, it is likely to be a bigger loss and you are likely to lose more of your own money.

I believe that when you are young and relatively poor it is worthwhile to borrow as heavily as possible. If things go well — and with property they do probably 80% of the time — then you will build up wealth quickly and efficiently. If you have bad luck ... well, you're young and there are still years ahead to have another go. However, as you get older the consequences of loss are greater. Early in my investing career, 80% of everything I owned, including my house, was financed with borrowed money. Now I have only 40% borrowed and my equity is the other 60%. As I have got older this change to conservatism feels right.

Each person has their own threshold of tolerance when it comes to taking risks. Taking risks beyond your own level of tolerance causes serious anxiety and is an unpleasant way to live. Nevertheless, to be a property investor you do need to be something of a risk taker.

The term *negative gearing* refers to the situation of a property where the rents are not sufficient to cover all the outgoings — so the property makes a loss. Negative gearing actually has more to do with measuring cash flows than with measuring gearing.

In the past, with high inflation a fact of life, it made a lot of sense to own properties that made a loss — even when they were fully tenanted. This was especially so when real interest rates (the difference between the interest rate charged by the bank and the rate of inflation) were low. It was advantageous to be negatively geared because property values more or less kept pace with the high inflation (i.e. the rate of capital gain was high), while the amount of money borrowed stayed the same. Nowadays, it is often difficult to borrow enough money to ensure interest payments exceed rent, and in any case the value of this is debatable. The question mark that hangs over negative gearing is: will there be sufficient capital gain to offset the costs of short-term losses? Incidentally, one of the effects of low inflation and low nominal interest rates is to bring many more landlords into the fold of the tax-paying classes. Previously, the main rewards of owning rental property came from capital gain, which was usually tax free!

Internal rate of return (I.R.R.)

This is a method for calculating the overall performance of a particular property if you own it. It is tailored to your financial situation, which for each person is unique. Thus it is seldom used by valuers because it is not normally an objective measure of worth — although it can be used objectively if borrowed money is eliminated from the calculation.

The internal rate of return is used by investors because investors are quite properly subjective people, concerned specifically with their own interests. The internal rate of return takes into account the borrowing of the owner of the property. It also combines the rental income stream with the capital gain (or perhaps capital loss) to generate a measure of performance over a period of some years.

Consider the following issues, which all vary between properties and owners, and with time:

The financial scenario. Each rental property has a unique set of financial particulars, e.g. rates, insurance costs, maintenance, the rate of depreciation on buildings and chattels and the timing of when it is claimable. Property also incurs costs when it is purchased and sold: real-estate, legal, valuation and bank fees.

Profit and loss. There are two outcomes with all rental-property investments. The property makes a profit or loss each year, and when you come to sell the property it will be worth more (or possibly less) than what you paid for it.

Taxation. Any profit or loss made by a rental property will be taxed at a rate that varies depending upon the overall tax position of its owner.

Inflation. This increases the cost of building new rental housing to meet a growing tenant population.

Supply and demand. Supply and demand for rental property may change over time and so alter market rent levels.

There is a lot of detail in the above considerations. A properly constructed internal rate of return analysis will consider all these issues, and assuming your guesses about inflation, rent levels and so on are correct, can be used to predict the likely future profitability of a rental property you may wish to purchase.

One way to understand I.R.R. is to pretend you are opening up an account at "I.R.R. Bank" using a large cash deposit. Visualise your property as a bank account. In our example (see p.20) the equity/deposit of $100,000 is the first deposit into the "I.R.R. bank". Each year the owner of these flats will either put some of their real cash into the I.R.R. account, (when the income of the rent is less than the expenses of the flats), or take out some money (when rental income exceeds expenses and a profit is made.) In our example, the latter applies — a profit of $8,550 before tax is made. When the property is sold in the future the owner will hope to get back their original $100,000, plus more as a capital gain due to the value of the property increasing. This is the same as closing the I.R.R. account and withdrawing everything that is there, both principal and accumulated interest.

With a real bank account the interest rate is typically calculated monthly. The more you put in, and the longer your money is in the account, the more interest you earn. The I.R.R. calculation takes the cash flows of each year and then works backwards to find the interest rate. The cash flows of each year include the first year when a large input was made (the deposit) and the last year when a large output was achieved (profit from the sale).

Usually, these days, the calculations of internal rate of return are done by computer. I have done this for our example of the four flats, using a computer. In doing so I assumed a 2% inflation rate and so increased all expenses and the rent by 2% a year, and also allowed the capital value of the buildings to grow at 2%. As per our example I allowed 7% of rent for management. Over a 5 year period the before-tax internal rate of return came out at 16.62%. This would be the same as investing the $100,000 in the bank at 16.22%.

At a marginal tax rate of 33% the after-tax rate of return drops to 10.87%. The after-tax internal rate of return is useful when comparing one property against another, because some property purchases are more "tax effective" than others. For example, you may have the choice of buying a large property with a lot of borrowed money, or a smaller one with less money borrowed. The larger property may have a tax loss in the early years, so you may get a refund of some of the tax you have already paid out of your wages for the year. This will mean the after-tax internal rate of return will be higher than the pre-tax rate.

When using an internal rate of return analysis be aware that this analysis includes no estimate of risk. Generally, the more money you borrow and the older and more dilapidated the property the higher will be its internal rate of return. Both these situations carry greater risk.

If you can use computer spreadsheets it is quite straightforward to set up one that calculates internal rate of return. The formulae for calculating I.R.R. are part of the software. Consult the software manual.

The business of buying a rental property

As well as calculating the numbers, in order to feel comfortable enough to make an offer on a property I need to know the current market conditions.

Getting a feel for the current market. What I mean is the rent levels, trends and the current ownership enthusiasm for the business. The market for purpose-built investment blocks of flats, for example, is more volatile than that of regular houses that are in demand among home-owners as well as investors. Just as the sharemarket is either in a bull or bear phase, so it is with investment property. However, with investment property it can be a little more difficult to ascertain the phase. As with the sharemarket, the best buys are made when you have the courage to buy when everyone else is keen on selling and prices are falling.

Talk to other rental-property owners and join the local Property Investors Association. Your local Citizens' Advice Bureau or a real estate agent should be able to give you a contact number. (For the address of the national organisation, see Appendix 1.) Like all non-profit voluntary organisations, their effectiveness varies from place to place and from time to time. Get their newsletter, go to their meetings and talk to people you meet there. If the local club isn't working so well, you could get involved and make it work better. There is a national residential-rental property magazine, *Estate*. Currently it costs $50 a year for a 4-issue subscription, or $7.50 a copy at bookshops. See Appendix 1 for the address.

As mentioned earlier, real estate agents are an important source of market information — especially for the current demand for investment properties. A source of information on the current demand by tenants for rental accommodation is professional property managers. These people typically work for real estate firms and you can often get an introduction to one through an agent.

Make the acquaintance of a valuer. When you do buy something, chances are you will need a valuation. Beforehand, however, you can go to a valuer and say that when you buy you will use him or her. Talk about the investment property market and what may have been recently sold, and get their opinion on trends.

Buying through real estate agent. When a property is listed for sale with a real estate agency, the individual agent in the real estate firm who arranges this becomes the listing agent and will receive a listing commission when the property is sold. The agent who finds the buyer gets a selling commission and the firm itself gets a percentage — and of course the government gets its GST.

Most areas of New Zealand are dominated by the exclusive listing system. This is where only one or perhaps two real estate firms have the right to sell the property. For many of the big firms, over 80% of their sales come from their exclusive listings. If you are dealing with one particular agent, he or she can often "work in" with another firm and access a particular exclusive listing of theirs for your inspection and purchase. Nevertheless, as a buyer wishing to know every property that is for sale of the type you are looking for, you really need to establish a relationship with a particular agent in *each* firm in town.

Get a card from each of these agents and keep them together. I suggest you ring all the agents once a month or so to keep your name in their minds. In the long run, if you consistently deal with only one agent in each particular firm you are likely to build up a relationship of trust and get better service. Also, watch the newspapers. If an estate agency is advertising for sale a property of interest to you, ask "your" agent in that firm why he or she hasn't already told you about it and get them to show you the property.

Private sales. Often these are found by responding to small advertisements in the "Properties for sale" columns of the newspaper. You can also access properties through personal contacts such as fellow investors you may meet at property investors association meetings. If you are interested in buying a property somebody owns, let them know: "sow a seed in their mind" by saying you would be interested in buying if they were ever wishing to sell, and ask them to contact you. You may also see local properties of the type you are interested in buying — particularly ones that are perhaps looking a little neglected. Find their owners by door-knocking — tenants usually know who their landlord is. Also, the Lands and Deeds Office and local councils have computer lists of all properties by street address showing the owner's name. You can usually then find the owner listed in the phone book.

When buying a property, particularly in a private sale, it is useful to get a private valuation done. (You will probably need one anyway if you are going to borrow money from the bank, so it is not necessarily a waste.) The valuation price of a property is normally the sale price and an agent's commission is deducted from this. Therefore, from this valuation (and your knowledge of the market) you can try to negotiate a lower price. Split the difference, so both parties gain.

However, with private sales the adage "let the buyer beware" particu-

larly applies. You need to be on guard for faults in the property. Real estate agents are fair game for being sued when a purchaser finds they have bought something different to what the agent told them it was. For this reason, agents are typically more cautious about telling lies. Buying privately, however, you are probably more likely to experience misrepresentation. On the other hand, by directly talking to the owner you can often gain much more in-depth information about the property.

Finding out information on a property. It is probably unrealistic to expect to find out everything there is to know about it. In the often rough-and-tumble of the buying process, assumptions are made and calculated risks taken. Surprises, some pleasant and perhaps some not, lie in wait for the new owner. This is particularly so of older properties. Nevertheless there are ways to gain knowledge about a property for sale. Two sources are the local council and the lands and deeds office.

Local body information. Local bodies usually have files on each property within in their jurisdiction. They also have and manage the city plan (called the district scheme). There is a deal of information you can get from the local body. For example:

- What building permits have been issued.
- What sewer and stormwater services there are to and on the property, and whether the drains are shared with any other property.
- What standard or special engineering conditions apply to the property.
- What zoning the property is and what uses are permitted in the zone.
- Whether any conditional uses or specified departures have been granted on or near the property.

- Whether the property is designated for any public work or amenity.
- Whether the council has any outstanding requisitions on the property, for example repair notices.
- What the rates are for the property.

To get this information from my local council there are two ways. Directly from a counter inquiry I can obtain details of what building consents and permits have been issued for the property. I can also get a photocopy of the sewer and stormwater layouts. To get more detailed information I need to apply under the Building Act for a Land Information Memorandum ("lim" for short). This application costs $50 and takes a maximum of 10 working days. The request goes to 6 separate departments of the city council and results in a complete disclosure of all information the council holds on the property.

Gathering information from the property's title. The Lands and Deeds Office is where you "search the title". This office is a branch of the Justice Department with an office in most cities. A title search costs $5 and you end up with a photocopy of the certificate of title. A title is what your lawyer will want to see before approving any purchase and sale agreement.

When land is transferred, it is recorded on the certificate under a reference number. By referring to the last transfer reference number you can get over the counter of Lands and Deeds, for your perusal and photocopying, the Memorandum of Transfer document. This shows the price paid. In the same way, using the reference numbers of any mortgages on the certificate of title, you can examine the mortgage documents and usually find how much money has been (at least initially) borrowed against the property. All this is public-domain information. These details of the owner's position are not necessary or even always relevant. However they can at times be valuable background information to know.

Sort out your ownership structure. Before making an offer on a property, you need to have done some planning to decide which form of ownership suits you best. Will the new property be in your own name, your spouse's name, in a partnership, in a company name, or will you have some other arrangement? Often the best professional to give this advice will be an accountant, as most of the decision-making in this area turns on the question of taxation (see p.15).

Some rental properties are owned by a company. You may be invited to buy all the shares in this company instead of the title to the land. This may suit you, to avoid tainting (see p.17). However, be aware that when you buy an existing company, you buy its liabilities as well as its assets. One liability is the accumulated depreciation on buildings claimed by the company to date. In the future when you want to sell you can likewise sell the shares in the company instead of transferring the title, and you won't have to pay the deprecation clawback tax either. However, as in the game "pass the parcel", ultimately the music will stop, somewhere down the line the property will need to be sold and the clawback tax paid. For this reason alone (not to mention the extra paperwork), company shares are generally less valuable in the marketplace than a clear title.

Viewing the property. Sometimes with multi-unit properties you don't get to look through each flat at the time of inspection. Don't commit yourself to buying until you have seen through each one. It is not uncommon for one or two units to be badly run-down; perhaps you have only seen the well-presented ones. When viewing rental property, also talk to the tenants. They are often valuable sources of information about a property.

Making an offer. To be enforceable, all contracts for the sale of land must be in writing. You cannot verbally buy a property. If you are dealing through a real estate agent, he or she will draw up a contract. Get your lawyer to check it out. When private buying, either your lawyer or the vendor's will have to draw up a purchase-and-sale agreement form. In either case, go and see a lawyer and discuss the implications of the offer.

A common condition is a "subject to finance" clause. This allows you time to arrange mortgage finance, and if you can't you are not committed to buy. A clause without this or any other condition is called a "cash offer". Cash offers are often more enticing to the seller.

At this meeting with the lawyer, ask what information there is on the title that may be important. There are a number of different title types, e.g. cross-lease, unit title, Glasgow lease. The description of these is beyond the scope of this book; get your lawyer to explain the implications of each. There may also be easements and other encumbrances on the title giving other people rights over the land. Discuss these and if necessary get further information from the Lands and Deeds office.

Auctions and tenders. Not all properties are available for "private treaty", the offer and acceptance system described above. Property auctions normally require you to have 10% of the price available as a deposit on auction day — and, of course, confidence in being able to raise the rest on settlement day. Banks will often give a commitment to loan to you before the auction — but this needs to be arranged. Often properties at auction are "passed in" and subsequent negotiations can include such conditions as "subject to finance".

With the tender system, you can put in such tender as you wish making it subject to conditions — such as the finance condition. Conditions, once again, tend to weaken the value of your offer, but they reduce your risk.

Mortgage finance. Most people reading this book will be home owners and have had experience with raising a mortgage. In the past, people tended to build up a relationship with a bank and do all their business with it, but nowadays it is a case of shopping around for the best mortgage deal. Loan-establishment fees may be negotiated downwards, and interest rates may vary between lenders.

Before shopping around, prepare two financial statements. The first one is an assets-and-liabilities statement showing everything you own and everything you owe (the difference between the two is your net worth.) The second is a cash-flow statement showing regular money in and expenses out for both your present situation and your future financial situation once you have purchased the new property.

The criteria you have to meet will vary. For example, a typical bank criterion may be firstly that the borrowing be no more than 75% of valuation or purchase price of the property (which ever is the lower). Secondly, that your income must be sufficient to pay the mortgage charges from 30% of gross salary plus 80% of gross rents.

Mortgage lending on commercial property has interest rates a percent or so above residential ones. Some banks classify all residential rental property as residential while others classify it as commercial. Still other banks are somewhere in between, e.g. in their criteria a four-unit property is residential while five and above units is commercial.

Lending criteria changes over time as individual lenders make decisions to become competitive in the market and so increase their residential lending or move the other way and decrease it.

Banks on the main street of your town are not the only source of mortgage finance. There are the banks that don't have branch offices but will nevertheless deal with you by phone, fax and letter. Other lending institutions to consider are building societies, trustee companies, solicitors' funds and insurance companies. Vendor finance is another source.

Here the seller lends some money, typically as a second mortgage. If this is an option for you, you need to find a first mortgage holder who will allow this.

The large number of competing lenders has given rise to the mortgage broking industry. These professionals will recommend and arrange applications to lenders on your behalf — and they usually pick up their fees from the lenders. I guess if you are very busy or don't know how to shop around for finance, a broker is worthwhile. It is just that to date I haven't used one. The old do-it-yourself kiwi in me still beats strong I guess!

Insurance

"Malicious acts by tenants or their guests" are not normally covered in insurance policies. In my town I know of three recent instances of this calamity. In one case a skinhead "flatmate" (in a house next door to one I own) smashed all the windows, gib board and internal doors, generating a repair bill of some $15,000; another tenant with an intellectual disability set fire to his rental property; and a tenant set fire to himself in a suicide in the ceiling space. In the last case the owner told me he was paid because the tenant's primary motive was to cause his own death rather than arson. But the other two, I expect, would not be covered. However, the Crombie Lockwood Group of insurance brokers (who have offices in the lower half of the North Island and Christchurch) have a special landlord's insurance which includes automatic cover for malicious damage by tenants.

Replacement insurance is where you get a new building in replace of an old one that has been destroyed. Because all insurance is tax deductable, I figure getting new in exchange for old (particularly if the old building sits tilting on the landscape like bait for a bulldozer — as one of mine does!) would be a bit like winning Lotto with the government allowing a tax deduction on the price of the ticket. Replacement insurance is the most common type of domestic insurance, but my insurance company won't give me replacement insurance in the above, rather extreme case — I can only get indemnity insurance.

Indemnity insurance (often called market-value insurance) in theory won't make you richer (or poorer) than you were before the damage. In the event of a claim you will be paid a sum of money equal to the cost of repairs or the market value of the building, which ever is less. In the case that old wreck of mine, for example, most of the money paid by the insurance company may be for a bulldozer and a dump truck to take it away, leaving a vacant site to sell. (It's probably worth more vacant than it is now with the old house on.)

The basic system of house insurance in New Zealand is that the company pays for fire insurance and a government-backed scheme called the Earthquake Commission adds on the natural disaster component to all fire policies. The Earthquake Commission will only pay out up to a maximum of $100,000 per dwelling unit. When you have got two or more flats on a property, make sure your insurance company knows this because if they don't, $100,000 for the whole property will be the maximum payout.

Taking over as the new owner

Usually when buying property there is a process of offer and counter-offer, followed by a period of conditional sale. Once the conditions have been met the point is reached where the deal is said to have "gone unconditional". Only at this point can you say, "I have bought a property." The contract will provide a date for settlement and possession. Now begins the phase of taking over as new owner.

Dealing with the existing tenants. In the purchase-and-sale agreement, you need to be clear whether you are buying the property subject to existing tenancies or whether you are buying it on a "vacant possession" basis. In the latter case the vendor will then be obliged to give the tenants 42 days' notice to leave. You may then approach any tenants you wish to keep on and sign them up as new tenants of yours as from possession date. The ones you don't want have to leave on or by the possession date.

Usually with existing tenants you will be buying the property subject to their tenancies. As new landlord you are taking the tenants over where the old landlord left off and are bound by the same tenancy agreement as before. If the vendor landlord, for example, allowed the tenants to keep a dog, then you are bound to allow this to continue. If you want to change this, you need to negotiate a new tenancy agreement. If the tenant won't willingly agree to the changes you want, you cannot impose the changes. Instead, you need to give 90 days' notice of termination of tenancy and from the end of the 90 days you can offer them the tenancy agreement you want. It is over to them whether they accept the new agreement or leave. (See chapters 4 and 5 for more detailed discussion of tenancy agreements.)

All rent is due to the vendor up to the date of possession and thereafter it is due to you. The changeover may be in the middle of a rental-payment period, and rent received in advance by the vendor is money due to you. This can be worked out by the two conveyancing lawyers and the difference incorporated into the settlement price. However, especially if one is dealing with a number of units, the changeover typically involves some untidiness and only relatively small amounts of money, so it may be best kept off lawyers' desks. One tenant may be late with their rent; another may not get their automatic payments changed over when they say they will, and so on. Ideally you want a good relationship with the vendor to sort out these issues as they occur.

Bonds paid into Tenancy Services by the outgoing landlord have that landlord's signature on the documentation. Tenancy Services have a form for use by landlords when the management of rentals changes but the tenants stay put. It is a yellow form titled "Change of Landlord/Agent". Arrange for this form to be completed and signed by yourself and the vendor, so your signature is now the one to authorise the release of the bond money.

Chattels inventory. Within the first few weeks of taking possession, draw up an inventory of the chattels and assign market values to them for the purposes of calculating depreciation (see chapter 7). Chattels are such items as the carpets, drapes, light fittings, electric stove, stand-alone fireplace, and so on. By itemising these and assigning market values to them at the time of purchase, you are in a strong position should there later be any dispute with the I.R.D. regarding their value. You were there at the time and noted their condition at that time. With rough tenant use they may well look less valuable to a tax inspector 18 months later — but he is 18 months too late.

Chapter 2

Making the decisions

Being a landlord creates the need to make lots of decisions. Some will be made on the spot, others after much thought and research. Some you will avoid and hope they will go away (they usually don't!)

Fixing up the outside or inside first?

There are two aspects to the presentation of a property: the inside and the outside. I believe tenants place a greater emphasis on the quality of the inside than the outside of the property, for the following reasons. When home owners buy a house, they are making a strong statement about themselves and their position in society. They will easily pay a two or three times differential between two buildings of the same quality but in different neighbourhoods. Tenants, on the other hand, are still tenants wherever they live and if they rent in a nice neighbourhood they are still renters rather than "position-taking" owners.

Of course they prefer to live in a better neighbourhood, but they are not willing to pay two or three times the rent for the advantage of doing so. Generally, what tenants are more concerned about is the quality of the inside of the dwelling — the size of rooms, quality of walls and floor coverings, and the fittings such as showers and taps for auto-washing machines. These matter more to them than the outside. Tenants lay out their furniture and possessions in their dwelling, this is what they own and this is what makes a statement about their position to their friends and others.

The upshot of this for you as a rental-property owner is that you should spend money on the inside of a property rather than the outside. However, when it comes to attracting a scrupulous and fussy tenant, attention to the presentation of the property from the road will pay dividends. It will minimise the number of tenants who will contact you from your advertisement, then drive past and keep on driving. Even if you have got the inside looking great and if they saw it they would take it, you haven't had a chance to show it to them as they have already been put off.

Do I do the work myself or pay somebody to do it?

Rental-property ownership allows flexibility with this question. For example, you may give the property to a manager for the purpose of collecting the rent and arranging tenancies, while you do all the physical work on the place. Alternatively, you can do the management and have a handyperson do all the work. Again, you can completely put your property in the hands of a professional manager while you pursue some other activity — perhaps an extended overseas trip. Some owners never do anything themselves and entirely leave the property in the manager's hands.

Nevertheless, in my opinion, unless you do most of the work yourself, residential rental is unlikely to be the best use of your capital over the long term.

You should at least do the management, most of the interior decorating and the basic maintenance such as replacing tap washers and electrical fuses. The basics of this are covered in chapter 8. Of course you can hire help for these tasks, but I believe you begin to lose your competitive advantage if you do. Most residential landlords are small-time, quick-on-their-feet, price-cutting individuals. Seldom do residential landlords gain large portfolios in New Zealand. Once the portfolios of the particularly successful ones begin to grow past the stage where they as owners can manage the properties themselves, the advantages of generally higher gross rates of return begin to be dissipated on higher management costs and (usually) longer vacancy periods resulting from overloaded management. At this point, it just makes more sense for the increasingly wealthy and time-pressed investor to invest in commercial and industrial property where less personal involvement is required relative to the amount invested.

Basic up-grades

There are two modernisations I have found well worthwhile in all my older properties: installing a shower and fitting automatic washing-machine taps. In most cases I plumb new showers in over an existing bath. The detachable shower that fits over the existing bath taps is cheap, but seldom worth it. Tenants don't like them as the temperature is hard to adjust. Moreover, they usually don't last long under the hard use a succession of tenants put them to, and being detachable, they may be stolen.

For washing-machine taps I like to plumb in a couple of brass water taps. These are inexpensive, reasonable quality and easily maintained. Although easier to fit, special adaptor taps are expensive, often difficult to use and difficult to fix when they leak.

Furnished or unfurnished?

It was commonplace in the 1960s and 70s for flats to be let with furniture. The first flats I bought in 1984 each had a fridge and washing machine. One of my first disputes with a tenant came quickly when the fridge broke down. I replaced it with a more modern one that — unbeknown to me — didn't have a large ice-chest. The old one had, and the tenants had been used to using it as a freezer. They didn't like not having a freezer, and claimed I had changed the conditions of the tenancy agreement by not supplying a freezer along with the fridge. Then the washing machine broke down. It wasn't long before that block of flats had no furniture at all, and for a long time I had no furnished flats. I remember another landlord saying, "After you've fixed the twentieth washing-machine pump on a Saturday morning, *then* you will give up the idea of furnished flats."

Then, about 8 years later I became aware that prospective tenants were often saying, "Is there a fridge and washing machine in the flat?" It seemed everyone else in town had given up on appliances in their flats as well, and there might be some market advantage in doing something different. By this time I had a basement under a block of flats with almost a household lot of furniture. As tenants had left over the previous few years they had often left an item or two behind. The more delinquent the tenant, the more it seemed they left behind. I bought a few new items, costing $600 in total, and advertised a "semi-furnished two-bedroom flat". It had a double bed and mattress, single bed and mattress, 2 chests of drawers, sofa, 2 armchairs, a vacuum cleaner, fridge/freezer, kitchen table and 3 chairs, and a washing machine. The rent was $15 a week more than the flat was worth unfurnished — or $750 a year, So for my $600 outlay I received a 125% annual return.

I also occasionally will fit a tenant out with the odd bit of equipment. I remember buying a couple of washing machines and a fridge from a school gala for $30, and they are still in use. If a tenant is looking at the flat and in discussion I find they are short of an item or two of household furniture and I have got it in my basement, then I will lend it to them and write on the tenancy agreement, "This is an unfurnished flat. The washing machine is on loan from the landlord to the tenant separate to this tenancy agreement. Should it break down the tenant may return it to the landlord without liability, or repair it at the tenant's expense." The advantage here is I can secure a tenant by offering these extras to get them settled, but not be stuck with the responsibility for keeping up the repairs.

Curtains

Curtains are pretty much the market norm and it would be difficult to rent a place without them. New curtains in a flat brighten it up. I make my own. This saves time waiting for a shop to make them, which can be an important factor, especially if the flat is vacant. (Actually, the sewing machine I have is one that was thrown out in the rubbish by an outgoing delinquent tenant!) I usually buy remnant material, although it is often difficult to get enough of the same to do the whole job. Also I keep a stock of curtains purchased on spec at garage sales and the like. Often I can just pull something out of stock that will fit. The fit needs to be in both size and colour.

When a flat is changing tenants I often take the curtains home and wash them. Curtains collect dust and cigarette smoke while they hang, and need a good clean occasionally. Washed curtains can be hung back up on the windows wet if there is not much time. Alternatively, drying them on a clothesline first and then ironing them perks them up a treat.

Curtain rails come in for a lot of abuse in flats. I go for the non- adjustable ones now. Made of a single aluminium extrusion, they tend to stay put better and last longer than the detachable, adjustable-for-length variety.

Lace curtains are good for where a window is facing onto a public area such as a path. They don't cost much. Unfortunately, they usually have a short life in strong sunlight, and cats and children pulling on them speed the process up. Tenants often supply their own lace curtains.

It is not uncommon for tenants to pull all the blinds shut and keep them that way. Usually this is a sign the tenant is in a depressed state. The flat may become dank and smelly as a result. I don't have any answer to this problem. If they are paying the rent and reasonably looking after the place, how they have the curtains is their own business. In extreme cases of mildew buildup some management intervention is justified.

The most important curtain is the one for the shower. There are some inexpensive ones on the market now, and it is these I use. I buy them a few at a time and always have one on hand. The price of a shower curtain is much less than the cost of replacing rotten floorboards, and some tenants will shower without a curtain from one year to the next if there is not one supplied.

Light bulbs, stove elements, chimneys and carpet cleaning

Whose responsibility are these? Should you replace blown light bulbs, or should the tenant? What about stove elements? Cleaning chimneys and carpets?

It is a condition of the Tenancy Act that the tenant must keep the property reasonably clean and tidy (see p.91). However, if you want the tenant to clean the carpets as a matter of course when they leave, or to have the chimney swept regularly, you need to make this a condition of the tenancy when they move in.

Personally I don't bother to do so. However, if the carpet is particularly dirty I will try and make the tenant pay for cleaning it on leaving — using the bond. Tenants normally replace light bulbs and seldom ask me to do so (except in the case of fluorescent lights, which I will replace if asked). A burned-out stove element is something tenants seldom feel is their responsibility and I take it as mine. You see, I believe the proper attitude in our consumer society is one of "customer service". Other landlords take a different view, and include these items as conditions on their tenancy agreements, placing the onus on the tenant. These are decisions you have to make.

Dogs, cats and other animals

In New Zealand there are two type of tenant: those with dogs and those without. When I was born in the 1950s there was only one dog in my suburban street, and that was a working dog kept by a stock agent. The first big dogs I remember seeing were when the police got their dogs. Now probably a third of the houses in that street have dogs — mostly big noisy ones.

Personally I don't like dogs, and as a landlord I like them even less. Dogs bark and defecate and often are physically threatening. A block of flats with little ground is seldom suitable for dogs. If you allow one tenant on special grounds to have a dog, it is a hard job to say the other tenants can't also have one. When signing up a tenancy I usually write "No dogs permitted on this property." Nevertheless, I do on occasion see some advantage in accepting tenants with dogs, and the reason for this has to do with the fact that tenants with dogs are heavily discriminated against. It is difficult to rent if you own a dog, and this means the discerning landlord can find good tenants in people who have well behaved dogs and are self disciplined.

If the property has some grounds and is reasonably separate from other flats and neighbours I may make a conscious decision and decide to allow a dog. I then often put the rent up $5 a week and advertise "a dog O.K.". I can expect to get the worst sorts of tenants applying — along with some of the best. So I choose carefully and in my experience will generally have long-term, careful tenants who manage a well-behaved dog. (The two tend to go together. At the end of the day, there are no bad

dogs, only bad dog owners, and the dogs themselves are never really the root of the problem.

A problem that occurs from time to time is for the dog-permitted tenant to have a friend with a dog who has nowhere they can keep it. So it gets parked at my flat because I "allow dogs". When negotiating the original tenancy agreement with a dog owner I write on in it the name of the dog. For example, "The dog Smooch is permitted to live on the property but no other dogs". I don't want my tenants running a boarding-kennel.

If you suspect a tenant is keeping a dog inside a property contrary to their agreement, but you are not sure, a silent dog whistle may help. These are available from pet shops, and if blown outside the dwelling will usually cause any dog inside to whine or bark.

Generally cats are O.K. The real problem is kittens, and the problem with kittens is if they have novice owners. A kitten is a wonderfully appealing little bundle of cuddles and fun, but if not house trained effectively it will urinate and defecate — typically in the corners of the room or in cupboards. I have had some experiences in this regard that are too gross to describe here. Use your imagination and be cautious in assessing cat owners.

When it comes to cleaning up after cats, there are some good smell-eliminating products on the market that work O.K. on cat urine. I am told that another problem with owning a cat can be stray cats entering when nobody is at home and urinating inside to claim territory. They get in through the cat door or a window that was left open for the cat of the household to come and go. However, I haven't had this problem myself.

In summary then: watch the kittens. You may want to write on the tenancy agreement, "No kittens under the age of three months permitted on the premises." If a kitten has survived to that age it is probably house-trained. With up-market houses you may well consider banning all pets except goldfish.

Hanging things on walls

Do you allow tenants to hammer nails into the walls for hanging up their dartboard? Actually, dartboards aside, the greatest problem I have in this area is with sticky tape holding up posters on painted wallpaper. When the tape is pulled off the paint comes too, leaving large unsightly marks. Blue-tack has much the same effect after it has been on a wall for some time.

I often think the difference between a plain unattractive flat and an inviting one (especially to younger tenants) is a good measure of posters on the walls. In other words, I'm not about to make so many restrictions that the tenants cannot hang up pictures and posters. Having permitted this, I encourage the use of drawing pins to attach posters to walls. They leave small holes — much less of a problem than the sellotape.

In a better-quality place you may want to restrict the driving of nails into walls. If a tenant hammers a nail into a wall it may be a big one — perhaps an old roofing nail. It may be driven into gib board without first looking for a stud. It will look O.K. while a picture is hanging there, but on its removal a hole will be left behind. But in most of my flats, I am content to put up with this. Nail holes are lot easier to deal with than the bigger ones made by fists or furniture slammed against gib board.

Especially if you have an up-market place, you may like to put a condition to the effect that only picture hooks may be used to attach wall hangings — and then attach them yourself after consulting with the tenant. You get to find the studs and the tenant gets the pictures more or less where they want them.

Dartboards need a large backing board — at least. Even then, damage from stray darts is likely.

Floor coverings

Nowadays, without reasonable-quality floor coverings you are unlikely to be competitive in most rental areas in New Zealand.

Carpet

A newly-carpeted flat is a transformed dwelling. Carpet is also great for soundproofing and warmth, and inviting to prospective tenants. It just calls out, "I can be your home."

Carpet can be expensive to buy and lay. The key word here is *can* — it need not be. This is especially true of more basic flats where second-hand carpet is acceptable. New carpet acquires a second-hand look soon after it has been laid, anyway. Probably if you buy new carpet it will be of the cheaper grade, but with prudent buying a second-hand carpet of heavy-weight quality will give a better life. The cost of laying carpet is the same whether it has got a lot of life left in it or only a little, so it is not economic to lay carpet that isn't going to last at least five years.

Nylon carpets are usually cheaper than wool and they wear better. They also get dirty more easily, but on the other hand are easier to clean. Nylon easily acquires burn holes where cigarettes have been dropped or sparks have jumped out of a fireplace; however, it is particularly serviceable in heavy use areas of hallways and door ways.

When re-decorating a flat I like to choose the carpet first. Often it is selected from my somewhat limited range of what I have on hand at the time. Once that decision has been made, although the carpet seldom is laid at this stage, the colour of the walls and the curtains can be chosen to match up.

What goes under the carpet determines how it will feel to walk on. Underlay is usually worth the cost, especially if you can obtain some second-hand. Often the underlay under the old carpet is O.K. to use again. Sometimes at a pinch I will lay the new carpet on top of the existing worn carpet, using the old carpet as an underlay.

Some of the best carpet I have ever got has been discarded or sold from commercial premises. Often it has come from a set of offices. Typically, there are worn-out tracks from doors to desks, with effectively new carpet left under filing cabinets, in corners of rooms and so on. It is a little more expensive to get a carpet layer to cut out the worn places and piece the good bits together.

Vinyl

Carpet in the kitchen is a headache. Spilt food soon turns it into something resembling a cowshed at milking time. Carpet in the bathroom is just waiting to soak up water and hold it there to rot the floorboards. So I use vinyl in these areas.

I like to use commercial-grade vinyl, put it on to a solid base. The quality of a vinyl job depends on the quality of the floor to which it is glued. As with painting, it is the preparation that determines success or failure. Smooth concrete, sound chipboard flooring, or closely-nailed heavy-duty hardboard on sound tongue-and-groove flooring provides the necessary base for a vinyl-laying expert to work on.

Electric ranges

Brand new, these are a thousand-dollar item. The great thing is that many home-owners like to upgrade their kitchens regularly by buying a new electric range, so second-hand stoves are plentiful and relatively cheap. There is little justification for a landlord to buy a new electric range. When buying second-hand stoves, I try and stick to one make and model, which has turned out to be the Shacklock 24. This way I only have to keep a very limited range of spare parts on hand, and with older types of stoves they can be obtained very cheaply. You can even whip them off old stoves at the rubbish dump if you're really keen!

I used to get lots of calls, particularly from new tenants, saying the stove had broken down. The problem almost invariably turned out to be that they had inadvertently activated the timer, causing half the stove to shut down. Nowadays I disable the automatic timer device by removing a key part. This saves a *lot* of bother. Timers are a fandangle gadget that nobody seems to use, anyway.

The worst thing with electric ranges is the oven being left filthy after use. A tinfoil tray under the bottom element, or at least a length of foil, makes a great difference and may save you cleaning it out next time around.

Lawns

Where a lawn is clearly part of the property the tenant is renting, you can reasonably expect them to mow it. However, in most properties you will probably have to supply them with a mower (usually a hand mower will do), because they are unlikely to have one themselves. You will need to get the machine serviced about every 2 years.

More problems occur with common ground. Where the lawn is common property between two or more tenants it is difficult to get just one of them to look after it. One option is to negotiate lawnmowing as a condition on one particular tenancy agreement, except that when the tenant doesn't mow it you have the problem of enforcing a breach of the agreement. (To help this, you may hit upon the idea of having two rents due. One rent if they mow it and another, higher one if they don't. But that won't work, because under the Act, the lower rental becomes the legal rental whether they mow the lawn or not — see page 109.) In the long run, the easiest solution is probably for *you* to deal with it — mow it yourself or pay a contractor to do it regularly. I prefer the latter course of action, and am still surprised at the modest cost I can get it done for. Other landlords welcome the opportunity that lawnmowing provides for regularly visiting the property, building up a relationship with the tenants and keeping an eye on things.

Gardens

Most tenants like looking at gardens and flowers, and an attractive garden helps rent out a flat. However, few tenants will actually work in the garden. Consistently in my experience, 7 out of 10 tenants will tell me, "I like gardening," but only 1 out of 10 ever does anything. Furthermore, of the few gardens that are started, even fewer are kept up, and when there is a change of tenants a weedy mess often results.

My conclusions are firstly that the statement, "I like gardening" actually means, "I like looking at gardens but have neither the tools nor desire to do the work needed," and secondly that tenants who do start a garden are more trouble in the long run than those who never do. Nevertheless, gardens run deep in my Kiwi blood and I have never yet been able to say "no" to anyone who wanted to start one.

Although these comments may sound rather negative, they apply mainly to the bottom two-thirds of the rental market. More up-market properties usually attract tenants who look after at least some of the gardening duties.

Weedkiller is my gardening friend. I get fired up with my kit about four times a year — in early spring, late spring, summer and autumn. I go around all my properties and spray weed growth in driveways, lawn edges, around trees and even inside gardens.

Agapanthus are useful, trouble-free plants. They take over an area and produce flowers. I have a few of them about.

You are probably more of a gardener than me, so I will leave you with your gardening problems and keep the rest of my prejudices to myself.

Chapter 3

Tools of the trade

Landlording is both an investment and a business. In this chapter we are firmly into the move onto the business side of the equation.

The telephone

The telephone is an essential tool for communication today. Make it work for you and don't let it become a master. For example, don't fall into the trap of staying home to take the calls just because you've placed an advertisement letting out a flat. Nor should you let your dinner burn while answering a call at an inconvenient time. Here are some suggestions to help you manage your phone.

The telephone answering machine. These are no longer the oddity they were only a few years ago. Nowadays people are much more confident about leaving a message on them. The machine has three functions — recording messages, leaving messages and call screening.

Recording messages. This is the basic function of an answer-phone. I have an answerphone and tenants can always get a message through to me — notice of leaving, repairs needed, rent not paid on time, and so on. If I want an early night I put on the answerphone, wind down the volume to silent operation and pull the plug on the phone. I never get disturbed all night and messages are there in the morning if anything important has happened. My machine also has a function enabling me to call in from any other phone and listen to messages.

Leaving messages. When advertising flats to let, I often change the outgoing message — for example, "If you are ringing about the flat advertised in the paper, It is 34 Valley road and I expect to be there working on it until 5 P.M. so come and have a look if you wish. Otherwise leave a message after the beep." Again, once the flat is let but while the advertisement is still running, I can change the message to tell callers, e.g. "If you're ringing about the flat, sorry, it has been let. Otherwise, you can leave a message after the beep." This saves me having to call people back.

Call screening. When callers leave messages on my machine and I am nearby, I can hear them talking. Sometimes, when busy I will leave the machine on for the purpose of call screening. Most calls I will let go onto tape, while I will answer calls that are about more urgent matters, or from friends. If I am advertising an up-market property I may let all calls go

onto tape and make some judgments from the voices before ringing them back. However, with very bottom of the market properties, I try and be on hand to take all calls as often many prospective tenants in this market segment are calling from telephone boxes and may not be able to leave a number where I can call them back.

Other telephone functions

The "call interrupt" facility, available from Telecom, enables you to know when somebody is trying to phone in while the phone is already in use. I, or other members of the household can have a long personal call to a friend and not worry that the phone is unavailable for incoming calls, for example in response to an advertisement for a flat to let.

Another facility is the call diversion. When I go on holiday I can divert all of my calls to a landlord friend who can attend to emergencies. I do the same for him when he's away.

List of tenants' telephone numbers

Shortly after a new tenant moves in, I ring Directory Service and find out whether they now have a telephone number. If my tenant is on the phone, I update the tenant telephone list which I keep on my computer and print out as needed. (Also on this list I keep the numbers of trades people I regularly use — builder, plumber, cleaner, electrician, etc.) I carry one copy of this list around with me and keep another on my desk. It is handy to be able to ring up a tenant rather than make a trip around to the property. This list also provides me with a handy reference of tenants' names if I ever forget them. Unfortunately, often the tenants that give the most trouble with paying rent on time also don't have enough money to keep the phone on.

Business cards

Having a card is a statement that you are serious about your business and professional in your behaviour. Get some made up — they are cheap enough these days.

Car

It is easier for tenants to relate to you, especially in blocks of lower-market flats, if they see you in the same sort of vehicle they'd drive, rather than for example a BMW which may encourage feelings of resentment. An older vehicle is also more practical for carrying around the tools of your trade as a landlord.

Computer

A personal computer with a printer helps you process financial data and produce professional-looking letters. I keep track of my financial affairs by using simple computer spreadsheets. I keep a week-to-week cash flow analysis. On another spreadsheet I record expenditure data ready for the tax return (see Chapter 7), and on a third spreadsheet I have an overall annual budget. With my word-processor function I am able to produce individual letters from standard ones to tenants covering such things as rent arrears, notices of inspection and so on.

Because the financial affairs of landlording are relatively simple, you don't actually *need* a computer. But if you do have one at home and don't know much about it, then landlording can be an easy way to get started with them. Once in use it is hard to imagine life without it.

Check account

In chapter 6 we discuss the opening of a separate rental-house bank account. Into this account your tenants will pay their rent and you will keep a check on them doing this. Get a cheque book with side-butts; it is easier to record the reason for writing out each cheque. An account with a bank that operates in "real time" is an advantage, as when a deposit is made to your bank account your account records this transaction immediately. The other system has an overnight delay.

The best news for landlords is telephone banking. If you only have a few rentals, simply phoning the bank's talking computer weekly will enable you to keep a check on rental payments. Having each of your tenants paying a slightly different amount is a great help here: see page 105. If you have more than a few rentals, a weekly statement with telephone updates as necessary will keep you right up with the play.

House maintenance tools

Chapter 8 deals with the various maintenance jobs needed around the house. If you are a do-it-yourself, home-owner handyperson then you will already own a range of tools that can also be used with your rental house. Otherwise you will probably use hired help for this.

Chapter 4

Selecting tenants

Choosing a tenant is one of the few times when I feel in full control of the landlord/tenant relationship. It is the time when I have the most power. It is much easier to stop a delinquent tenant causing me trouble by never allowing him (or her) into the property in the first place.

Nevertheless, the worst thing about tenants is when there aren't any. The most stressful times for me are those times when the rental market turns to an over-supply of property and vacancies occur. My expenses continue unabated while income may drop on some units from 100% of budget to zero.

There is a story of two hikers in the jungle confronted by a tiger. One of them digs out of her pack some running shoes and puts them on. Her companion says, "Why are you doing that? Don't you know you cannot out-run a tiger?" She replies, "Yes, I know, but I don't have to outrun the tiger, I just have to out-run *you*."

The market place is a bit like a jungle, isn't it? Why not get competitive and smart. Let other landlords have the vacancies while you keep a full house. It's often a matter of working a bit harder to get through the rough patches to enjoy once again the benefits of steady tenant demand. A systematic approach to the job of tenant selection is the most fruitful.

Towards a tenant selection policy

I have a policy, but as a sailor alters the sails to suit the breeze so I alter the trim of my marketing and selection procedure to suit the market. One winter about three years ago in my town the market went quiet. I remember talking to a man who had rung me up, and when I found he was staying with friends and had no transport, I said, "I'll come and pick you up and show you the flat if you like." It was a good chance to get a closer look at him at the same time. After looking at the flat he wanted it — but he had no money. I said, "The bond I normally have is two weeks' rent, however if you can only get $200 from the Income Support Service I will consider renting you at that amount of bond." I was taking a risk, but it was a calculated one. He, his partner and child turned out to be O.K. tenants. When they left 6 months later, the market was again strong and it was back to business as usual with my tenant selection standards and procedures.

The process of getting a suitable tenant kicks into action when one of the existing tenants gives notice, and ends when a new one is signed up and settled in. You need to develop a system for tenant replacement that works for you; that takes into account your resources and needs. If you work full-time, for example, tenant selection will probably have to be done only after business hours. Again, if you live on site the arrangements for viewing the property will be different from the situation of the owner who lives in another town; and so on.

The business of replacing outgoing tenants can be described in nine steps.

1. Prepare the property for re-letting.
2. Advertising the vacancy.
3. Deal with the advertisement's respondents.
4. Show the dwelling.
5. Check tenant references.
6. Offer the tenancy.
7. Collect the bond and sign up a tenancy agreement.
8. Fill out a property inspection report.
9. Write a letter of welcome.

1. Preparing the property for re-letting

I expect at least a week between when I advertise a flat and the new tenant moves in — often longer. Many tenants who are free to move into a flat straight away are under pressure to get out from where they are living. Often this is because they have not kept up their obligations. They are likely to repeat this behaviour with me. The more organised tenant is most likely to have a lead time between looking at a new rental and moving in.

Most tenancies in New Zealand are "periodic" (see page 85.) This means tenants are required to give 21 days' notice of a termination. The typical way notice is given by my tenants is by phoning me. Often they tell me they want to leave in less than 21 days. Even when they do give 21 days' notice I ask for more details. Often then I learn they would prefer to leave before the 21 days. In either case I remind them they are obliged to pay 21 days' rent. However, if I can find a suitable replacement tenant to move in sooner, they may not need to pay rent for all this time. It therefore is in their interests to help find a replacement tenant. This is a basis for working together.

I have an idea how each of my tenants live in their flats. Some live tidily, with the house spotlessly clean, displaying attractive furniture and wall hangings and with a smell that reminds me of romance and perfumed gardens. Others live dirty: they are untidy and have little in the way of furniture or decorations, and a smell that reminds me of wet dogs and compost heaps. Most live somewhere in between, and are prepared to spruce up for visitors.

A property that is well presented with a tenant's household effects will rent better than an empty flat. An empty flat, however, will rent better than an untidy/dirty one. It is hard work trying to change people. I have in the past given lectures on the regular cleaning of houses — but for so little reward that I have virtually given it up. With the incorrigibly untidy and/or dirty properties I prefer to show them vacant — after they have been cleaned. In order to lengthen my "life" as a landlord I have made a rule to avoid the depressing job of cleaning dirty flats. I have a cleaning person who will do a professional job at $14 an hour and when a vacant flat needs cleaning I get her on the job — and I hope to recover her expenses from the outgoing tenant's bond (see pages 87-89).

If you have a block of flats all the same and the one becoming vacant has rough tenants, you may be able to arrange with an obliging tenant in a tidy, attractive, identical flat to show prospective tenants through that one. You can offer the vacancy to a suitable tenant subject to the tenant inspecting the actual flat after it has been vacated, cleaned out and repaired.

Tenants are typically more influenced by the inside than the outside of a property, but a bit of attention to the presentation of the property from the road may be necessary to encourage tenants to come on inside and have a look. For example, I recall having a vacancy in a block of flats. There was a car wreck at the front of the block belonging to the tenants in the front flat. The car was painted red, and what wasn't missing was dented like a trampled-on beer can. The tenant had for some time been talking about a mate of his who was to come and tow it away. I didn't like the chances of his mate's promise coming off any time soon. I negotiated with the tenant that I would pay the $40 removal fee charged by the local wrecker, and he need only repay me $20 on his pay day. The car was picked up by a truck with a crane on it that afternoon and my block of flats instantly looked attractive again to new tenants.

Legal obligations

Legal obligations set the minimum standard. In order to be competitive in the market place you will usually need to have higher standards than that.

Under the Tenancy Act (s.45) the landlord is obliged to (1a) "provide the premises in a reasonable state of cleanliness" and (1b) keep "...the premises in a reasonable state of repair having regard to the age and character of the premises and the period during which the premises are likely to remain habitable and available for residential purposes."

So you need to have the property reasonably clean and tidy. However in the case of run-down premises that are due for demolition, under Section 1b there is little obligation to repair them beyond the basic standards.

The basic structural standards of dwellings are provided for in the Building Act. These are generally only enforced when a building permit is obtained for their construction, although in some towns the local authority enforces a system of regular inspections of "apartment" houses. They are:

1. You need to have a stove that cooks food by both boiling and baking.
2. You also need hot water in the bathroom and some form of heating in the living room. (Many of my flats do not have any fireplaces or heaters. If I am ever asked, I can give the tenants a plug-in electric heater.)
3. If the house is intended to accommodate more than two persons, you need adequate provision for washing clothes.

The smell of the place

The first breath of air your prospective tenants take as they come through the door of the flat may well decide for them whether or not they will feel good about living there.

I carry a can of air-fragrance with me. If I'm showing a flat to a tenant I like to get to the place first and check out the smell. If it is suspect I spray about. Often it is worth cleaning the carpets, and using a deodoriser, just to change the smell of a flat.

The worst problem I have ever encountered is dog urine inside a house. In bad cases the only effective solution seems to be removing the carpets, sanding the floor and re-sealing with polyurethane, followed by new carpet and underlay.

2. Advertising the vacancy

You can locate tenants through letting agencies, the local newspaper, referrals from outgoing tenants (or others in the neighbourhood who notice a vacancy coming up), and notices in local stores or public noticeboards, or a sign on the flat. Another possibility is a fellow landlord who has recently had a vacancy and generated a list of applicants from an advertisement. The first two of these are the most common.

Letting agencies are where tenants apply or look at lists of vacancies and the agent matches the two up. The agent does not manage the property and you are still left with the final selection. Nobody runs a letting agency in my town, although I did set up in the business myself once but it turned out to be too much work for the income. In bigger towns there is usually a letting agency. Normally the tenant pays a fee for their service and the landlord gets it for free, but in times of tenant shortage this is likely to change as tenants find they can easily get flats for free through the newspaper.

Referrals are when the outgoing tenant refers friends of theirs, or other tenants in the block recommend somebody. This is a characteristic of a "tenant-oversupplied" market. Watch that you are maintaining your standards — you can end up with less desirable tenants if you always accept referrals. Also, where friends of existing tenants are being referred, a refusal may offend. Advertising is a better way of testing the market response. Referrals from outgoing tenants do, however, have the advantage that the incoming and outgoing parties will sort out a lot of the changeover details themselves.

Notices on notice boards are worth trying, especially if you are operating in an environment where your potential tenants read notice-boards, e.g. a student area.

The newspaper certainly is, for me, the most important. There are two columns, the "wanted to rent" and the "to let" columns. The tenants who advertise themselves are better organised, more professional types, generally looking for something of good quality. When I read the "wanted to rent" advertisements, there are only likely to be one or two out of a full column that are looking for, or will accept, the type of place I have to rent. I am still likely to give them a ring — it is easy to do and something might come of it — however, this method in practice seldom produces results.

Advertising in the to-let column is a more certain proposition. As soon as a tenant gives notice to me, typically I advertise the property myself in the local paper. I get about 95% of my tenants this way. The wording of the advert is important: on the one hand I like to keep it brief, as it costs by the word; but on the other hand I want to explain enough about the property in order to ensure the only people who call are those it will suit. The advertisement is in fact the first stage in my selection process. Here's an example:

> **TWO BEDROOM** flat
> in a block, Broadlands,
> lockup garage, sunny,
> no dogs, $139 plus bond.
> Phone 5488553.

This advertisement gives the location, price (including the bond which, subject to negotiation, will normally be the standard 2 weeks' rent), adequate description, the main restriction (no dogs), and also gives the "plus" that the flat is sunny, which will count a lot in the winter. All this in just 17 words.

The people who *won't* ring are those who don't want to live in Broadlands, or in a block, or who have a dog. I like it that they don't ring up, because it saves me both time and the feeling of rejection each time prospective tenants turn a place down.

I like to describe in my advertisements the property as it is — warts, good points and all. I want to tell it as it is and not waste my time with applicants who would never take it anyway. For example, I might word the advert "One bedroom basic city flat $110 no dogs." At the other end of the scale if I have an up-market house and I must have top class tenants then it's "Two bedroom executive house available only to careful tenants..." which makes a statement of the property's position in the market, and my restrictions — without being discriminatory.

3. Dealing with respondents to the advertisement

Your initial response to an inquiry is, often, a good opportunity to do some quick tenant selection.

When an advertisement is placed in the newspaper there are two ways readers may be invited to respond: by letter (e.g. "Reply to advertiser 237," or by phone.

The write-in invitation is suitable where the market is particularly strong and there are many tenants looking for rentals — or alternatively when you have a bargain-priced rental and will therefore get many replies. When I bought my first flats there was a wages, prices and rent freeze imposed by the government. It is reckoned that 22,000 rental units were lost from the nationwide rental market over this period as owners gave up the business. (Rent freezes are a bit like neutron bombs in reverse: they destroy the rental houses but leave the people intact and desperate for shelter.) The rental market consequently had a severe shortage of supply and the write-in advert was one way of preventing experiences like one friend of mine had — 54 telephone replies to an advertisement in one night. Instead of that disruption to my household, I got a whole bunch of fan mail — as many as 24 letters to one advertisement.

However, in a more normal environment the letter write-ins cannot compete with the immediate response available by telephone. Answering back to the advertisement's applicants therefore comes down to answering the telephone. If you are not always going to be home, you will need a telephone answering machine.

Practice making judgments based on voice. Trust your intuition. For example, I often say to somebody I feel intuitively is "over-qualified" for a property, "Go and have a look at the flat and if you want it you can have it." I cannot recall ever having one of these people coming back to me and wanting the place.

On the other hand, perhaps I have had a few inquiries that have resulted in takers (people who want the rental) but I haven't made a final decision. If I get a caller who I judge as unsuitable I may say, "Sorry, it is gone — there are other people who want it." What I am saying, though not in so many words, is this: "There are plenty of other people who want the flat and I will make a decision from the other applicants I have... and I can tell by your slurred speech, the racket of your stereo in the background and your greeting, `Gidday mate,' that you don't stand a chance on this particular property anyway."

Note that anti-discrimination law is contained in the Residential Tenancies Act and the Humans Rights Legislation (see p.64). In practice, this legislation means you need to allow each applicant to "make application." You need to do this at least up to the point that you have made the decision to offer the rental to a particular applicant. If you make your judgment against a tenant too soon, e.g. by saying,"No, sorry: I wouldn't rent the flat to you anyway so you might as well not look at it," then you run a grave risk of having acted in a discriminatory and illegal way.

4. Show the dwelling

When preparing the property for re-letting, make plans for showing it to prospective tenants. This is the most time-consuming aspect of the whole deal, and often the most frustrating. The worst part is probably the non-shows — people who say they will come but don't.

There are five ways of allowing interested tenants to look at your property.

Let the existing tenants show the new ones through. Arrange this with existing tenants first. When tenants ring and give notice I talk to them about how I will arrange to show people through and often I will discuss the options of this method with them. It works particularly well if the outgoing ones have an interest in a quick re-letting and they keep the premises in a tidy order . This method is also easier to organise if the existing tenants have a phone. What I do in these cases is when people ring up and I want them to have a look through, I give them the telephone number of the existing tenants. I ask them to simply phone to arrange a suitable time to view. Also, I give the existing tenants an occasional call to keep them up-to-date with how things are going at my end, and get some feedback from their end. If the prospective tenants like what they see, they ring me back and that takes us onto the next step. If they don't like the unit I usually never hear from them again - although the outgoing tenants are often able to give me some feedback as to why not.

Leaving a vacant property unlocked and asking them to have a look through. There are some obvious security risks here. I ask the applicants for their name and contact phone number before I tell them the address of the dwelling. This reminds them I know who they are if they are tempted to steal something while on this unescorted tour. I use this method only with the more basic type of unfurnished rental unit — never on an up-market dwelling. In all the years of doing it this way, however, I have only had two problems. A detachable shower unit over a bath was stolen once. It was worth about $100. The second was when the unlocked flat became used by a vagrant who must have slept there a night or two and made a bit of a mess. For all the effort saved over the years, however, this method has served me well and is still in use — but I usually try to get there and lock them up overnight now.

When describing the location of a rental, give the address and also something else to go by "It is a red house with a purple letter-box", or "it is the second door up the drive way with flat 2 written on the door". Once again if the prospective tenant doesn't like the property I seldom hear from them again, but if they do want it they ring back.

Asking them to come and pick up the key and take themselves to look at it. This is a system commonly used by rental-management firms. They often use a form that is filled out and they also take a deposit on the key — to encourage its return. When the prospective tenant turns up I get a look at them and can draw some conclusions. Sometimes when they do turn up I will change my mind and go with them to look at the place — usually in their car to save the expense of mine, and have a chance to have a chat.

Making a time to meet them there. This is probably the most common method for private do-it-yourself landlords. Applicants ring in response to the advertisement. Those whom you wish to take their applications further, and those you find it difficult to give the "no" message to (given the anti-discrimination law), you invite to visit the property. To save time you will typically have two or three or perhaps as many as 10 applicants who want to have a look through. If the demand gets beyond about 10 I start telling callers the flat is probably going to be let, that I am not showing any more people through but that I can take their telephone number if they wish and get back to them if it still remains vacant.

You can choose to have separate times for each to visit — about 15 minutes apart is best. Or you can just give them all the same time. The problem with the 15-minute method is the "no-shows": people who just don't turn up for their appointed time. This is likely to be a bigger problem for a property that is poorly presented from the road, or at the bottom end of the rental market. I think they just drive by and keep on driving, or else they realise, after talking to you, that they want something better. the other problem with this method is that they often don't come punctually, so that applicants become bunched up. Giving them all the same appointment time cuts down on your waiting around for the no-shows. Often if I get a 50% show I'm doing O.K.

Once, when renting a flat I made the point of telling every caller that I had a lot of response to the advertisement and there would be a lot of other people coming as well. Also, I didn't take names of applicants. Well, out of 12 applicants who said they would come, only one showed up — and she seemed O.K. so I rented it to her. What had happened, I believe, was they thought there was little chance of getting it in the great rush and they gave up.

5. Check tenant references

You are under no obligation to take on any particular tenant. Some tenants believe it is a case of "first in, first served". They are wrong. Others believe those with the greatest need are entitled: with the most hungry children for example. Wrong again. Some existing tenants believe they can upgrade as of right — but there is no such right (although if they are scrupulous tenants it is in your interests to meet their needs to stop them eventually going somewhere else.) Sometimes I get previous tenants coming back and expecting me to think kindly of them — when in fact they were poor performers. (Maybe it was my nice smiling approach as they departed that gave them the wrong impression!)

The point is, you are under no obligation to make a fast decision, or any particular decision — and it is something I have to keep telling myself: slow down and do a thorough job. A bad tenant selection leads to a whole host of work and often worry down the track that can be avoided now.

Like all rules, it seems, there is the exception. In times of tenant shortage it pays to sign up quickly the first suitable tenant that comes past. In this situation there are many advertisements in the paper and few takers. Tenants enter the market and a smart operator will suss them out quickly. I recall a time both myself and a fellow landlord had an advertisement in the same paper for similar flats. He had a number of applicants to his better flat and I had fewer show up to mine. He took applications from them all, and after making his decision found in the two days this took his first choice had already signed to another landlord and the second on his list was also signed up — this time to me! He was left with having to accept someone who was a third or fourth choice.

The application form

Rental property managers use them for the, at times, endless stream of tenants coming in to look for rentals. However, private landlords (including me) seldom do. I think we do it to our disadvantage. There are many forms in use for this purpose. **Appendix 2** (page 143) is an application form you may consider using.

A psychologist once told me, "The best guide to future behaviour is past behaviour." Hardly needs a psychologist to say it, does it? Nevertheless, I need to remind myself of it whilst standing in a stream of tenants promising improved future behaviour.

For example, in this industry we cater for a lot of people on the move. The reason somebody has chosen to move, for example, is sometimes, "I want to shift out of my existing flat and come to this nice one to get away from all the problems back there and make a quiet life for myself here." This explanation, or anything close to it, sets alarm bells ringing. It appears to me the problems they "leave behind" must actually go into a dormant phase — perhaps in their luggage somewhere — so that shortly after settling in the problems leap out like stowaways at the end of a voyage.

You see, I just don't expect people to behave differently in my flat from how they behaved previously. So what I like to do is see references. Even better, I like to ring up their previous landlord/landlady and ask three questions: Do they have a good record of paying rent on time? Was the property undamaged and clean when they left? Are they considerate to neighbours?

Occasionally people ring me up for this information, and I always tell truthfully how it was for me. Whenever I have rung up, I have always got information that has stacked up. No doubt an unscrupulous tenant can arrange for a friend of theirs to be on the other end of the telephone number they give as their last landlord — perhaps in bigger cities this confidence trick is easier to arrange — but I have never experienced it. When I ask for the contact number of their last landlord the question itself usually sorts out tenants. Those with poor histories either lie about previous tenancies, which can't be verified, or they just wander off to find an easier landlord to get a flat from.

Income check

A phone call to their employer (if they're employed) is a quick way of checking that what they have told you about having a job is true. Smaller firms usually tell me straight off — they know their employees. With bigger firms, after I have explained to the personnel department staff who I am and why I want the information, they will look up their payroll records for me.

Credit check

Bay Collection Agency operates a centralised credit checking service (see Appendix). At the time of writing their charge for a one-off inquiry into the credit record of a private individual is $20. However, for clients who register and pay $40 annually it is only $9 per check. All these prices are plus GST. Information may be given over the phone and followed up by a written report.

6. Make a decision on applicants — offer the tenancy

Decisions are not always easy to make are they? For example, I had a large 3-bedroom house, there were a lot of inquiries and I showed about 10 people through. The "top" three (all professional families) did not want it — it wasn't up to their standard. That still left 7 people who did. One was a woman currently staying at the women's refuge and who had only just for the first time in her life left her home with 3 young children. I judged her to be of character, and she had a great need for the property; however, I chose a working class couple in their 30's. Both of them had jobs and were currently living in a one-bedroom flat. They intended to move in and take in one flatmate/boarder — who was also working. I rang up their current landlord and got a suitable recommendation. In other words, they did not have such a great need but were simply bettering themselves in the rental market. When the solo mother rang back, I told her no. She wanted to know why, and as we discussed it she decided I had made a financial rather than a moral decision. I think she was right. The three working people had a combined gross income about five times the rental, while she had only about two and a half times.

One thing she said (and it is often said by domestic purpose beneficiaries) was that the income support service would guarantee the rent. This is not true for us private landlords. Except for Housing New Zealand, who can get direct rental payment from ISS, all of the benefit is paid into the applicant's bank account and from there they themselves must pay the rent. On tight budgets there are other competing demands for the rent money and it takes a deal of skill to make it all work. Nevertheless, although legally and financially correct I was left with a feeling of having done wrong by her, morally.

Discrimination

There are a number of things you are not allowed to take into consideration when choosing tenants. Anti-discrimination laws are enshrined in the Human Rights Act 1993 and expressly forbid any form of discrimination on the following grounds:

- sex (which includes pregnancy and childbirth)
- sexual orientation
- marital status (you cannot specify "married couple")
- religious or ethical belief or political opinion (you cannot advertise for a "Christian" tenant)
- colour, race, ethnic or national origin
- disability (including physical impairment or psychiatric illness)
- age
- employment status (i.e. being unemployed or on a benefit), and
- family status (i.e. whether you have children).

If a tenant takes action against a landlord over illegal discrimination they may choose to use the Tenancy Tribunal or the Human Rights Commission, but not both.

So what *are* you allowed to use as criteria on which to base your selection criteria? Here is a list.

Ability to pay
Dress (including gang patches and shaven heads)
Number of occupants
Pets
Smoking
Drinking habits
Number of vehicles and type of vehicles (e.g. noisy motorcycles)
References from previous rentals
Noisiness
Cleanliness
Honesty
Waterbeds

Of course, when you turn down a prospective tenant for any of these reasons, they may accuse you of doing so for one of the prohibited reasons. For example, in the case mentioned earlier, the woman from the refuge probably thought I was concerned that her children would be troublesome in some way, or that I was not prepared to take that risk. However, my decision hinged solely on the question of her ability to pay.

Illegal discrimination is commonplace in our industry. An experiment was done in Auckland. Two women of identical age, standard of dress, income, family status and references approached rental managers, separately but on the same day. The only difference between them was one was Maori and the other Pakeha. The latter was invited to view a number of more up-market properties that the Maori woman never got told about.

To some extent we as rental-property owners cause some of our own problems when we discriminate against a particular group. Everybody needs to sleep. The question is where do you sleep if you belong to a discriminated-against group? The answer is they usually bludge accommodation from those members within the group who do have accommodation. This leads to overcrowding, which in itself is a good and real reason for owners to exercise discrimination. So a vicious circle is created.

For example, I rented a one-bedroom flat to a pleasant enough young chap who turned out to be a punk rocker. I got to know a fair bit about him and perhaps 30 or so others that made up that particular sub-culture living in our small town. Their music was weird, unpleasant to me and often loud. They lived in the pattern common among young unemployed, of staying awake until the early hours of each morning and sleeping in late. There was a condition on the tenancy agreement that occupancy was limited to 2 persons but my tenant would tell me, "How can I tell them to leave at 2 a.m. when they have got nowhere to go — they can't get landlords to rent them flats." One day at noon I was told by a "guest" who answered my knock on the door that there were 16 others still asleep. This in a one-bedroom flat! Such numbers make heavy demands on my toilet system, stove, front door and carpets (they never took their big boots off). My tenant didn't like this overcrowding either, but to reject them would be somehow to reject the support of his group — something he would need when I evicted him — which, of course, I eventually did.

I find the young unemployed kiwi male the most difficult class to house and am cautious about all-male households as tenants. Young men often have few of the skills needed to run a household on their own. However, it is of course sexual discrimination to make a distinction on this basis.

Having a choice among competing applicants is preferable to having no applicants. Whether or not to leave it empty if there are no tenants meeting your eligibility criteria is a decision I hope you don't have to make. With the up-market properties I manage, I will leave them empty rather than take a risk. In the more basic flat, loss of rent is balanced against the risk of bad tenants. Shortages of suitable tenants may be seasonal in some cases, e.g. where there is a student accommodation demand that falters in the summer. At other times it seems to just be a vagary of the marketplace — a bit like the weather. As such, storms are followed sooner or later by sunny periods. One landlord told me it usually comes down to "do I lose money up-front keeping it empty and using my time and money advertising, or do I lose it down the track with defaulting tenants and perhaps the expense of repairs?"

Of course there is always the question of rent level. Lower the rent enough and you will let a flat. Often just $10 a week is enough to make a big difference in demand. (See p.103)

Make your decision. If it is "yes", make sure you only say it to one applicant. At all times, be clear in your own mind and communicate clearly exactly what stage you are at in the process of entering into a contact.

In order for a contract to exist there has to be an offer followed by an acceptance. You make the offer and invite the tenant to accept. There are two forms of offer: the simple offer and the option.

6. Offer the tenancy

A common situation I face is having a suitable tenant to whom I want to rent my property. He or she is willing to sign a tenancy agreement but doesn't have any money there and then. I don't feel safe until I have some of their money. What I do is offer, for a defined time, the tenancy to them on condition they pay the bond. I make this offer in writing. **Appendix 3** (p.144) is a form you can use for this purpose. I tell the applicants they can change their mind before the time (usually about 24 hours) expires, but I cannot. If they don't show at or before that time I assume they don't want it and I will offer it to someone else.

In the case of the tenant looking to Income Support Service for their bond money, this written offer has the advantage of being acceptable documentation. ISS will give the tenants a letter of approval and a few days later I will receive a government cheque in the mail, or a direct payment to my bank account.

If you are unsure how committed the tenants are to accepting your offer, or if the offer period is a long one, then you may consider using an option. This requires the tenants to pay some non-refundable money in order to "buy" the right to sign a tenancy agreement. (See **Appendix 4**, p.145.) Section 17 of the Act limits the amount you may charge for an option to one week's rent, and stipulates that when the tenant exercises the option the money must be refunded or applied to the rent. The advantage to you is that if they don't exercise their option, you get to keep the money — some recompense for the trouble and lost opportunity they have put you to.

7. Collect the bond and sign up a tenancy agreement

I don't like signing up a tenant without a bond. Often this presents a problem, for example if the tenant already has a bond tied up at the property they are vacating. Often I will ring the landlord of the vacating property and if what I hear reassures me that the tenants are likely to be able to retrieve their bond, I will take the risk and negotiate on the basis of a bond transfer soon after them taking up the tenancy. It is a risk, though.

Bond

A bond is defined in the Act as "any sum of money payable or paid under a tenancy agreement as security for the observance and performance of the tenant's obligations under the agreement or this Act: but does not include any sum payable or paid by way of rent." (See pages 73-74 for more on bonds.)

I was once told there are two types of tenant: those who are starting a tenancy and those who are ending one. At the beginning it's all smiles and agreement, but relationships do not always end that way, and a bond is a good way for me as a landlord to maximise the number of happy endings. Most of my bond claims are for rent arrears, with cleaning and repairs second. For example, recently I talked to a young tenant of mine who was paying the rent irregularly and had fallen into arrears. I found he had over $5000 in outstanding debt. Half his mail was from debt collection agencies and the interest and collection fees were growing at a greater rate than the debt was being re-paid. Worse still, he had recently lost his job because he had cut his arm with a beer bottle one Saturday night. The only income in the household was from his girlfriend's low wages. Financially, the household was sinking. In the one hour between my ringing them and visiting them, they had faced their problem and arranged to split up and move back to their respective parents' homes. The bond I held plus a quick re-letting of the flat enabled me to avoid joining the end of his list of creditors.

A few rental property owners object to having to pay bonds to a government organisation, and on principle no longer collect them. I almost always collect bonds. When there is a dire shortage of tenants, there is a temptation to lower or eliminate the condition of bond, in order to attract a tenant. However, I still normally prefer to lower the rent and still collect a bond.

Between different towns the market average for bonds collected may vary. In Nelson, for example, two weeks' rent is the norm. To ask for more is possible (the maximum under the Act is of course four weeks' rent) but meets with resistance as tenants are not accustomed to paying more.

Signing up the tenancy agreement

Here you and the tenant are negotiating the boundaries of a new relationship you are both creating. Don't rush the process. I like to discuss and answer all questions as I go through the document, filling it in systematicaly and only moving on to the next point when I am satisfied we both have the same understanding of what we've agreed upon.

A tenant cannot give up any of his or her rights given by the tenancy act (s.11,3). This is because an act of parliament has stronger legal status than any contract.

For example, a tenancy agreement may be written up "The rent is payable fortnightly in advance and notice can be given two weeks either way." When it comes to the crunch, though, if the landlord wants the tenant out in 2 weeks, the tenant has the right to stay put. The landlord can only give the 90day/42day minimum notice as set out in s.51. Notwithstanding this, the tenant can take advantage of this clause in the contract and only give 2 weeks' notice. This is because, unlike the tenant, the landlord can, and in this case has, signed away the right to 3 weeks' notice. (See p.87.)

On the other hand, the Tenancy Act defines many of the tenant's responsibilities. For example, even if you have an agreement that makes no reference to noise, a tenant who disturbs the neighbours with loud music is breaching section 40(c) of the act which states the tenant "shall not cause any interference with the reasonable peace...of any other person residing in the neighbourhood."

In my opinion and experience, long elaborate tenancy agreements are of dubious value. They may even be disadvantageous, as shown above with the "two weeks either way" example. The basic set of rules are in the Act and there is little scope for operating outside these rules. The standard tenancy agreement form provided by Tenancy Services is a good one to use. See Appendix 1 for the address of your local office.

Using the standard tenancy form

The 1996 amendments to the Act mean the Tenancy Service's agreement will need to be updated. Unfortunately this has not been done at the time of revising this book so I have to try and predict what the (probably minor) changes will look like.

In the first box the landlord must provide the tenant with a full name, an *address for service* and a *contact address.* The address for service is "the address at which notices and other documents ... will be accepted by or on behalf of the landlord" (s.2(1)) (see page 99 for more). "Contact address" is "an address or addresses (which may include telephone numbers) where the landlord or the landlord's agent is reasonably contactable by the tenant" (s.2(1)). If the landlord is a company then the name and contact address of the officer responsible and the address of the company's registered office must also be supplied. In most cases the address for service and contact address are the same: where you live. But it is up to you whether you give your tenants your telephone number. Some landlords may be concerned about possible nuisance calls.

In the second box the tenant provides the same information. Where "the tenant" is more than one person you have a partnership of tenants. The more names on the agreement, the more control you have over the tenancy, because when one of them wants to leave they need to come to you for a new agreement. However, it creates more work for you, because with large flats or houses rented by young people there is typically much coming and going of flatmates. Each time you have to reorganise the paperwork, including the bond. With more down-market properties, I work a system of "head tenancies". This means I have only one or perhaps two names on the tenancy agreement — people I've judged suitable to take a leadership role. If the head tenant leaves, the whole agreement is up for re-negotiation, and I will only sign up another head tenant I feel I can equally trust.

At the other end of the market (better quality properties) I usually go for partnerships so I do have control over who lives there. For example, in a 2-bedroom house I may let it to a young couple, but if she leaves and he stays and maybe gets in one or two of his mates as flatmates I have a totally different household. By having both their names on the agreement, if she wants out of the contract, I can demand an empty flat. Also with partnerships, if something does go wrong (such as damage, rent arrears) then any person on the agreement can be sued for the entire amount of the loss. The legal term for the liability of partners to third parties is "jointly and severally". The term "severally", means that you can select the most creditworthy tenant (or ex-tenant), or the one that is still in town, or the one you have managed to track down to where he has moved to, and go him for the entire amount. The term "jointly" means that if, for example, none of them is creditworthy, and you believe you may have a better chance of getting a little from each (or you feel it only fair to do so) you make a claim upon them all. In this case each of them may be ordered by the tribunal to pay you their share directly.

Note: *When signing up a tenancy agreement with a partnership it is worth writing the term "jointly and severally" after the names to make it plain to all, and discuss this aspect with the tenants at the time of signing.*

The tenant must supply an address for service and a contact address. Usually, these will both be the rental's address, but it can be advantageous for this address to be different from that of the rental property, because if at the end of the tenancy you want more money than you held as a bond (damage, rent arrears, etc.), then your chances of getting it improve if you have a quick way of finding where the tenants are. With young people it is often a good idea to ask for their parents' address as the address for service. The workplace of a tenant with a steady job may be another suitable address. (In fact, as I wrote this I realised a tenant of mine had left 4 months ago and I hadn't signed anything to do with his bond, which he is entitled to get back. However, I had his work address as an address for service, and so was able to send him some good news!)

This address for service must be a street address, not a box number. If the flat address is used, get whatever other contact addresses you can (parents, work address, etc.) and keep a record of them. (See p.99.)

Usually the tenant will not have a phone number at the time of signing. I put their current contact number in here, or their parents' number. After they move in I'll write in their new number here (in a different coloured pen, to show it has been added after signing).

The third box is for details of the property itself. The address (easy) followed by "Furniture, etc. provided by landlord (if any)". With unfurnished flats I write a brief descriptions of chattels, such as "curtains, floor-coverings, light fittings, stove". With fully-furnished properties, it is usually necessary to have an inventory attached. In the case of owners going overseas, for example, and renting out fully-furnished houses, some of these lists grow to being a mammoth job in themselves. A careful home-video camera record of the details of every room is probably a better alternative. There are commercial companies who do this work — usually for the purpose of creating an insurance record for a house-contents policy. They will do one for you for a fee. They keep the tape in storage, where it is available as evidence if need be in the future.

The next part of the form comes below the third box:

The landlord and tenant agree that:

1. "The tenancy shall commence on..." This is the date from which the rent flow begins. It is a date often calculated forward from to find the date up to which rent is paid. This is also the place on the form to identify whether the tenancy is fixed-term or periodic (see p.85.)
2. "The rent shall be $....per week/fortnight." I negotiate a rental payment period that fits in with the way the tenant receives income. If they are on a weekly benefit or a job that pays weekly then rent is normally paid weekly. If they receive income fortnightly then rent is paid fortnightly on the day they get paid. I also write at the end of this line the day of the week that rent is due, "on Thursdays" for example, or fortnightly on Tuesdays for a DPB beneficiary.
3. "The rent shall be paid weekly/fortnightly in advance." Easy: cross out one.
4. "The rent shall be paid at the following place or into the following bank account number." (See pp.104-106.) Negotiate the way the rent will be paid and write it in here. For example. "ANZ Bank # 010702 0138039 02", or, "paid in cash to the Valley Dairy."
5. "The tenant shall pay a bond of $..." Here you write the amount of the bond agreed upon. In addition, you will have to fill out the bond lodgement form. Mention of the bond here makes its payment a condition of the tenancy agreement, therefore its non-payment becomes a breach of the agreement (for example if the tenant's cheque bounces or a transfer from the previous tenancy fails to come through).
6. "The tenant shall not assign (transfer) or sublet the tenancy without

first gaining the landlord's written permission." It is advisable to cross out the last part of this sentence, so it reads "The tenant shall not assign (transfer) or sublet the tenancy." Under section 44 of the Act you are now expressly prohibiting the tenant from passing on the tenancy to somebody else. If you cross the whole sentence out the Tenancy Act actually enables the tenant to do exactly what the sentence says, i.e. assign or sublet — and furthermore, you cannot "unreasonably withhold consent".

7. "The tenant shall pay the solicitor's fee (if any) or the real estate agent's fee (if any) relating to the grant of this tenancy." There is a lot of work in selecting a new tenant and arranging the lease. If a member of either the legal or the real estate profession does this work they can charge the tenant for it as an up-front fee. We have to do the same work but cannot charge. On the other hand, these professional managers often have difficulties attracting tenants in a tight market, and so may have a higher vacancy level because they are charging their client tenants a fee that we aren't.
8. "This tenancy is subject to the Residential Tenancies Act 1986." This makes it clear that this is not an exempt tenancy under section 5 (more about this on page 84).
9. "Other conditions of this tenancy." This often becomes a much-used space on many of my tenancies. For example, "No dogs", "maximum occupancy is 4 persons", "First part-week's rent of $68 is due on 1/11/92, the first regular weekly payment of $140 is due on 5/11/92." "The driveway to be kept clear at all times." "On vacating the premises the tenants are to pay for all the carpets to be commercially cleaned." "The current water meter reading is 34430 and the tenant will pay for water used."

The bond form

The next task is that of filling in the green-coloured bond form (available from Tenancy Services).) The rules about bonds are:

1. They are optional.
2. No more than the equivalent of 4 weeks' rent.
3. A receipt is to be issued to the tenant upon recipt of the bond, showing the address of the tenancy, the amount and nature of payment (cash or cheque), the date of payment and name of the payer.

4. You as landlord are responsible for paying the bond to the Bond Processing Centre, Box 50445, Porirua. The Residential Tenancies Regulations 1987 prescribe the payment form to be used and this includes provision for the landlord's and the tenant's signatures. Occasionally I forget to get the tenant's signature on a bond form at the time of signing up a tenancy and have sent in a bond form without a tenant's signature. The form has been accepted but if I want to claim some of the bond money it is ineffective to have the tenant sign the bond refund form. The bond centre doesn't have the tenant's lodgement signature to compare and so it is treated as a "one-party claim" which takes longer to process (see p.88, 89).

Even if the tenant does sign the lodgment form, there are times when the tenant's signature is not recognised. For example, with the young couple who got into debt (see p. 68), we had agreed for all the bond to be paid to me as rent arrears, however he had his writing arm encased in plaster from the beer-bottle incident. He signed the refund bond form with his free hand, but the bond office couldn't recognise the signature and so treated my application for a refund as a "one-party claim". I had to wait about a month for the money to be paid out.

Personal guarantees

Third party guarantees are an opportunity to have somebody other than the tenant guarantee the performance of the tenant. When you and a tenant sign a tenancy contract, you are the first party and the tenant or tenants are the second. The idea is that some third person who is more creditworthy than the tenant, can come into the contractual process and underwrite the tenant. Usually in our business, the third party is one of the parents of the tenant. Many university and polytechnic students, for example, are financially supported by their parents and a personal guarantees formalises this support.

Appendix 5, p.146, is a personal guarantee form which you may find very useful in this situation. It provides a guarantee of performance in the "observance by the tenant of all their responsibilities contained in the tenancy agreement". If the tenant gets behind in the rent, for example, usually a phone call to the person named on the personal guarantees will result in some action.

If it comes to taking legal action against a guarantor you cannot use the tenancy tribunal. For claims involving sums under $3000 (and between $3000 and $5000 when both parties agree) you can make a claim to your local Disputes Tribunal, otherwise it is off to the District Court.

Keys

The tenancy agreement gives the tenant legal access to the property; now you have to give physical access. It is important always to have a set of keys yourself for your rental premises. Tenants sometimes lock themselves out and ring up for a key. Occasionally, tenants drift off at the end of a tenancy and take the keys with them, in which case I normally just get new ones cut. Some people consider there is an obligation in this situation to change the locks for the incoming tenants. I seldom do. I figure if the outgoing tenants are going to be burglars, they can just as easily get a new one cut before they leave and hand in the old ones anyway.

I have a big key ring about 150mm in diameter with all my landlord's keys on it. The keys to each place are ringed together and labelled. I only write the street number of each residence on the label — leaving off the street name just in case the big ring is ever lost or stolen.

I like to give the incoming tenants at least two keys, and three if I can, to the front door (or the door they will most usually lock when they go out). The reason for giving them plenty of keys is because I advise them to hide an emergency key somewhere outside. This strategy reduces the emergency callouts I get. It is a good idea to note on the tenancy agreement the number of keys given so that on termination you will get them all back. In fact often I get more back, as tenants cut extras while they are there.

8. Fill out a property inspection form

Often, when I point out a defect in a property (a fist-hole in gib-board, for example) the tenant will say, "That was here when we came." What is really helpful in these situations is a record of the condition of the property at the start of the tenancy. Tenancy services have a property inspection report form for this purpose.

The proper time to fill this out is after the tenants have signed up but before they move in. Often, however, I fill it out on my first inspection, which takes place within the first month of their moving in. By the time they have had a couple of weeks living there and paid the rent once or twice I like to see how they live. By this time they have also have had a chance to discover any problems with the property, for example a window that doesn't lock tight, a blocked chimney, a place where the roof leaks in heavy rain. New tenants are quick to point out faults that I can get on and repair. More established tenants, however, often don't bother to report such problems. They probably think they may be blamed for the fault, or are accustomed to living with the fault and don't want the intrusion of the owner, even if he is only repairing something.

So I make a time to inspect the property, (see page 90), and while I am going through the property fill out one of these sheets and get their signature on my copy.

9. Letter of welcome

After the tenant has settled in and paid the first rent (perhaps by automatic payment), I like to send them a short note saying, as well as the pleasantries:

"Your first weekly rent payment of $114 came through into my bank account by automatic payment on the correct date of 7th October — so the system is working well. If you have any problems with the rental let me know. All the best."

Communication is a two-way thing and this is my way of saying, "Hello and welcome; I am getting the rent okay at this end, thank you and keep it up."

Chapter 5

A guide to the Residential Tenancies Act

The 1986 Residential Tenancies Act was history-making stuff when it was introduced. Now we have all got used to it and it is part of the paintwork, as it were. This act has created three entities that are significant in the life of a landlord: the Bond Processing Centre, the local tenancy service offices (and mediators), and the tenancy tribunal. We start this chapter by discussing each of these and then examine the legal rights and responsibilities of landlords as defined in this Act.

The Bond Processing Centre

In the normal day-to-day administration of rentals this is the entity you will have most to do with. The Bond Processing Centre receives and pays all residential-rental bonds in New Zealand. It is situated at Porirua, near Wellington. For their address and toll-free number see Appendix 1.

The forms to use when signing up tenants and paying money to the Bond Processing Centre can be obtained from the Centre by mail, or from your local Tenancy Service Office.

Local Tenancy Services Offices

Throughout New Zealand there are Tenancy Service Offices (see Appendix 1 for their locations). They have three functions. Firstly, they offer free legal advice on tenancy. They generally know their stuff and you can rely on the advice they give. Most of this advice is sought and given over the phone. Secondly, they act as the office of the Tenancy Tribunal. This means they do the work of organising Tribunal hearings. This brings us to their next function: thirdly, they provide a mediation service.

Getting your case into the tribunal system

In order to take a particular problem with a tenant beyond the simple seeking-of-advice-from-the-tenancy-officer stage, and on to mediation and or a tribunal hearing, you need to fill out a blue form from Tenancy Services that bears the title "Application for Order of Tribunal".

The first part of this application form deals with simple details such as landlord and tenant names and address for service. In the next part you are asked to write down what you would like the tribunal to do for you. An example of what I might write here is: "Terminate the tenancy, award possession of the premises to the landlord and make an order for rent owing."

The next part of the form asks the reasons for this. Here I might write: "The rent is only paid up to 1 November. It is now 23 November so the tenant is more than 21 days in arrears."

A provision for a date and a signature complete the form. Once the tenancy office gets the form, it and any attached documents of evidence are likely to be photocopied and given to the tenant.

There are, in my experience, three courses of action the tenancy office may do when they get an application. They may contact the tenant by phone and try to negotiate an outcome; they may arrange a mediation session, or they may set a date for a tribunal hearing. In any particular case they may do one, two or all three of these — but not all at once.

If a mediation session is organised, and both you and the tenant are willing to attend, this is how it works. You will meet with the tenant and a mediator (who may or may not be the same person who gave you any advice previously). These meetings usually take place at the offices of the Tenancy Service, in a small private room with comfortable chairs around a low table. Any agreement you and the tenant come to will be written out by hand on a special form by the mediator, signed by both parties, and a copy is given to each of you. You may present your copy to the office of the tribunal within six months and they will, except in exceptional circumstances, arrange for the tribunal to "seal" it with a big rubber stamp. Once stamped it has the full legal force of a tribunal order (see later).

The basic rule is that anything said in mediation is confidential and does not represent evidence for a tribunal hearing. There are, however, somc cxccptions to this rule. For example, where both parties agree that certain facts are true, and with the consent of both, the facts may be written down by the mediator in a report for the tribunal. The mediator may also report to the tribunal on the conduct of the parties, e.g. that one party failed to show up without a reasonable excuse, or that they acted in a contemptuous or improper manner. I can't recall a case where, provided that the tenant appeared at the appointed time and place, we failed to come to an agreement in mediation. It is a remarkably successful system.

You are likely to find a mediated settlement preferable to one imposed by the tribunal, for four good reasons: in some regions there is a long waiting list for tribunal hearings; it saves the time of appearing before a tribunal hearing; you may find the courtroom setting of the tribunal stressful; and there may be more chance that the tenant will abide by something they have "agreed" to rather than something "imposed".

However, if it is a matter not available to the mediation process, or if one party does not agree to attend or fails to show up, or the mediation session fails to reach agreement on all the points in dispute, then it is on to the next step — a tribunal hearing.

The Tenancy Tribunal

The Tenancy Tribunal is administered by the Justice Department. You will get a notice, usually personally delivered, giving a time, place and a photocopy of the original application. The notice of hearing states the following five points:

1. The parties to this application may agree to a settlement before the hearing, in which case the office of the Tenancy Tribunal must be informed as soon as possible.
2. You may apply to the Tenancy Tribunal for the issue of a witness summons.
3. Bring with you to the hearing any documents relevant to the application. These may include accounts, rent books, receipts, photographs, witnesses, copies of tenancy agreements, etc.
4. If you do nothing and do not attend the hearing the application may be heard and determined in your absence.
5. Any order made by the Tenancy Tribunal is final and binding on all parties and may be enforced as a judgment of the District Court.

The place you are likely to be called to appear at is a room at your local courthouse. Only in special circumstances (such as exceedingly complex cases or where one party has a disability) is a lawyer allowed into a tribunal hearing. In most cases you and your tenant (if they show) will be there conducting your own cases. The "judge" of a tribunal hearing is called an adjudicator, and is assisted on the day by a Justice Department clerk. Hearings are open to the public (unless in any particular case the adjudicator decides otherwise) but rarely do news media or members of the public attend. The proceedings are recorded on a tape recorder. You, and anyone else who gives evidence, will be asked to promise to tell the truth and warned that failure to tell the truth may result in prosecution.

The normal procedure of a tribunal hearing is to hear evidence, after which the adjudicator writes out by hand an "order" or decision, in triplicate. This is then read out by the adjudicator, stamped on each leaf with the seal of the Tribunal, and each party is given a copy. The document will order one or the other or both parties to do something. These orders are enforceable by the District Court (see p.99 -102).

To get the best possible outcome for you at the hearing, prepare your evidence well. The case will be decided upon the facts presented on the day.

The Act gives the tribunal leeway to accept whatever forms of evidence it chooses to, including accounts for repairs, rent books showing dates paid and rent-paid-to dates, photographs of damage, witnesses such as neighbours, copies of tenancy agreements, etc. If witnesses will not willingly come you can, in important cases, arranged for them to be summoned, meaning they *must* attend. The ability to accept any evidence it chooses extends the tribunal's scope beyond that of most other courts. For example, in one case I stood up and said, "The neighbour of the adjacent flat has told me the music is so loud at times windows shake in their flat." In this case the tribunal chose to accept my evidence as reliable and truthful because I appeared credible, but such hearsay evidence would be inadmissable in the District Court. (In a District Court the actual neighbour in person would have to come and say that.)

The philosophy behind the tribunal is the pursuit of natural justice in a flexible and informal way. The strict rule of law need not apply in situations where the merits of the case indicate otherwise.

Re-hearings and appeals

Either one of the parties may apply within 5 working days for a re-hearing (s.105). The grounds for such an application are that a substantial miscarriage of justice has been done. Where the adjudicator has awarded something that does not involve money or involves more than $1,000 you can appeal to the District Court. If you are still not happy you can appeal on matters of law to the High Court and then on to the Court of Appeal.

Is the Tenancy Act and the tribunal system fair to landlords?

I personally believe it is. However, rental-property owners often have the view that the tribunal is pro-tenant. There are probably three pillars of support for this view.

Firstly, the Residential Tenancies Act is a piece of social legislation. (It was arguably the only piece of social legislation put in place during the first term of the Roger Douglas government.) A lot of the support for its introduction came from liberals wishing to correct the perceived "natural power imbalance between landlord and tenant." (They mean the landlord is powerful.) You may think this is rather an astonishing view, given that the tenant actually lives inside your valuable capital investment, which can be wrecked — and they have the power to disrupt other income-producing tenants of yours in the neighbourhood.

Secondly, it is a piece of consumer legislation. You are providing a service and the tenant is the consumer and so has certain rights. These rights are in turn your obligations. In feudal society tenants owed loyalty and service to their master/landlords. In western consumer society this is turned up the other way and the consumer is king.

Thirdly, there is the question of even-handedness. In 1993, 87% of all applications made to the tribunal were made by landlords against tenants and 60% of all applications made were for rent arrears. These statistics suggest that tenants are mostly at fault. However, one of the tribunal's motivations is the desire to come up with a decision that both parties will in some sense agree with rather than being driven strictly by how the rules of law apply to the facts as presented and then going on to impose its will relentlessly. Therefore if the landlord has done something wrong in law it is likely to be given greater weight by the tribunal, than a similar wrong done by the tenant. The landlord's wrong is something the tribunal can seize upon to in some measure even up the balance of wrongs.

The landlords who do O.K. at tribunal hearings are those who conduct their business in a professional manner and strictly to the rules of the Act. You have to know the rules and behave as a landlord in a way that if any rules are broken it is the tenant doing so and not you. One mistake on your part is probably worth about 5 or 10 mistakes on the tenant's part.

Nevertheless, rather than any perceived landlord bias, I believe that the real injustice to landlords occurs where, because of overloading, there are long delays before hearings. Most tribunal cases are initiated by landlords for rent arrears. If the landlord is forced, for example, to wait six weeks for a hearing, a tenant in occupation has the opportunity to compound the wrong by an extra six weeks of rental default.

A metaphor for the legal aspect of the business of residential-renting might be a game of rugby. In renting, there are two opposing sides (landlord and tenant), a set of rules (the act), and a referee (the adjudicator). The referee can award penalties for infringements, just as a rugby referee can give free kicks at goal to the other side as penalties against you. In the game of landlord verses tenant, however, there are more penalties available to be awarded against the landlord than the tenant. There are two sorts of penalties. The first are "exemplary damages". If so ordered by the tribunal, these are sums you pay to the tenant. The second lot are fines, payable to the Justice Department.

Summary of exemplary damages (s.109)

$3,000 maximum: Discrimination (s.12)

$1,500 maximum: Seizing goods as payment of rent (s.33(2)); harassing a tenant (s.38(3))

$750 maximum: Requiring key money (s.17(3)); requiring excess bond (s.18(4)); failing to issue a receipt for bond or to pay bond money to the Ministry of Housing (s.19(2)); requiring more than 2 weeks' rent in advance, or requiring rent before the expiry of rent already paid (s.23(4)); changing or removing locks without the tenant's consent (s.46(3)); entering into a transaction which is designed to contravene, defeat or evade the Act (s.137(2)).

$150 maximum: Requiring payment of rent in excess of the "market rent" as determined by, and for the duration of, a tribunal order (s.27(2)), failure to give a written receipt in respect of a cash payment of rent (s.29(5)); failing to keep proper records of payments of rent (s.30(2)).

Compared with this list, there are only two for the tenant: changing or removing locks without the landlord's consent, and failure to allow the landlord to enter the premises when he is entitled to do so (s.48(4)): both $750 damages (s.46(3)). It would be nice to have a few more. One example that comes to mind is where I have signed up a tenant who enters into a contract with the condition "no dogs". Then shortly after they have moved in I find a big dog living there. It takes time and often game-playing by the tenant (hiding the dog) before I can get rid of the animal. There is not even any penalty to discourage the tenant from doing it all over again somewhere else — perhaps even to me again.

Fines and imprisonment

These penalties are applicable equally to tenant or landlords.

$1000 maximum: Failure to answer a witness summons (s.110(1)); resisting removal from a tribunal hearing after having been ordered to do so for contempt (s.112(2)); obstruction of a tenancy mediator in the exercise of his powers (under s.99) to inspect premises subject to proceedings in the tribunal and when requested to do so by the tribunal (s.114(7)); (All these fines are paid to the Justice Department.)

Up to three years' gaol: Giving false evidence to the tribunal (s.111). (This penalty can only be awarded by a district court judge.)

The Act (rules of the game)

The rule book for the game of tenant versus landlord is the the Residential Tenancies Act. It is 95 pages long, and as acts of parliament go, it is easy to read. A copy costs about $12-13 and can be purchased from Government bookshops. It is worth buying your own copy.

Looking for loopholes in the rules is counterproductive. It is not worth your energy listening to somebody who seems to have a clever idea "to get around the rules." The rules are clearly stated in the Act and the referee is fit, up with the play, and ready to call foul and order one of the numerous penalties available to be awarded against the landlord side.

Tenancies excluded from the Act

There a list of 22 tightly worded exclusions. I won't go into them all. One of the most important exclusions is s.5(n) "where the premises continue to be used, during the tenancy...as a place of residence by the landlord." This excludes the situation of flatmates or boarders living in an owner's home. Hostels and dormitories also are excluded (s.5 (h)).

However, the fact that you are reading this book means you are most likely in the category of a regular type landlord or landlady and the act is unlikely to let you out of its clutches.

Tenancy agreements

"Every tenancy agreement shall be in writing and signed by both the landlord and the tenant"(s.13(1)). It is the landlord's responsibility to arrange this before the tenancy commences (s.13(2)). However, if you accept rent from somebody living in a property of yours and you don't have a tenancy agreement (written or verbal), you are automatically setting up a "tenancy at large". The Act applies and the tenant still has all the normal rights such as length of notice, etc.

I sign up tenants using the standard Ministry of Housing form available from either the bond centre or local Tenancy Services offices. I have two copies, the second one made by carbon paper, and the agreement is signed by both of us. (See p.69-73 for much more on tenancy agreements.)

All variations to tenancy agreements likewise need to be in writing and signed by both the landlord and tenant (s.13B). This can create some work as often a tenant will ring up wanting to change some detail of the agreement (cg. the keeping of a new pet). The most straightforward way is to visit the tenant with your copy of the tenancy agreement and alter and countersign both the original documents. Alternatively, you may arrange an exchange of letters through the mail so that your and the tenant's signatures both appear on the same document of variation.

Minors

The Minors Contracts Act 1969 gives persons under the age of 18 the status of minors and as such they cannot necessarily be bound by a contract — including tenancy agreements. The tenancy tribunal, however, can agree before a tenancy starts that a minor shall be treated as someone of "full age". Any tenancy agreement signed by a minor becomes valid upon their turning 18 or marrying.

Periodic tenancies

The term "periodic" refers to the common type of tenancy, which starts on a particular date and goes on indefinitely until the tenant (or perhaps the landlord) gives notice to end it. This is the type of tenancy you have if you simply fill out the standard tenancy form step by step.

Fixed-term tenancies

A fixed-term tenancy has a definite end date. Under the Act, the tenant is required to quit the premises at the end of a fixed term. It is not uncommon for the tenants simply to stay living there after a fixed-term tenancy has run its term. If this occurs, they are in breach and the tribunal can order their removal. However, while they are living there they are still bound by all other conditions of the fixed-term tenancy (such as paying the weekly rent, looking after the place and so on). If you do absolutely nothing about re-negotiating their tenancy or having them evicted, then after 90 days the tenancy automatically reverts to a standard periodic tenancy (s.60(2)) and, for example, if you want them out you will have to give the standard 90-day notice.

The intention of a fixed-term tenancy is to bind the landlord and the tenant to keeping to the deal for the length of time specified. Furthermore, the rent cannot be increased during a fixed-term tenancy unless there is provision in the tenancy agreement for this. In practice, however, fixed-term tenancies are great for binding up the landlord, but there are a few holes there for the tenant to escape through. What do you do if the tenant's life-plans change and they need to leave before the term has expired? Also, sometimes, the owner of a house who has gone overseas for 2 years, for example, rents out their house on a fixed-term basis, but comes back home a year early.

The breaking of the term (usually by the tenant) is the most common issue with fixed-term tenancies. Section 66 allows either party to the agreement to apply for a reduction of the term of the agreement, and the Tribunal may grant such a reduction "where it is satisfied that, because of an unforseen change in the applicant's circumstances, the severe hardship which the applicant would suffer if the term of the tenancy were not reduced would be greater than the hardship which the other party to the tenancy would suffer if the term were reduced". In making this change the Tribunal may also make an order that reasonable compensation be paid to the disadvantaged party.

When renting a typical investment property in a normal market, most scrupulous tenants naturally hesitate to commit themselves to a fixed term. Most of the best tenants applying for a flat in a block of flats, for example, will only sign up with a periodic tenancy and if you insist on a fixed term, particularly one longer than say 3 months, you are likely to lose them.

I leave fixed-term tenancies to cases where they naturally coincide with both the tenant's and the landlord's best interests. For example, with student rentals, it may be a good arrangement for both parties, to sign tenants up for 12 months starting from the end of one student year. The student tenants may be willing to pay over the summer (even though they may not need the property and the landlord is likely to find it hard to get any tenant), in order to be guaranteed it for the coming academic year. If they do break the tenancy, they are more likely to be doing so near the beginning of or during the academic year. This is a time of stronger demand, and usually the property can be let at a higher rental. Thus it can actually be to your advantage as the landlord if the fixed term is broken by the tenant. Furthermore, with student tenants it is common to have personal guarantees from their parents, who usually are creditworthy people.

Again, in the up-market rental segment, large creditworthy companies rather than individuals may take on a fixed-term tenancy for their employees. In any case, you are typically dealing with creditworthy and long-term planning tenants and the odds are that the fixed term will work O.K.

Waiver of rights tenancy

The Act gives both landlords and tenants rights and powers. As previously discussed, any agreement that a tenant makes to forego a right "shall be of no effect" (s.11(3)). The inability of a tenant to contract out of the

Residential Tenancies Act is a key element in achieving the act's purpose — paternalistic protection to the disadvantaged tenant class!

The landlord, on the other hand, can voluntarily give up rights (s.11). For example, if the property is sold or the landlord wants to live on the premises, he has the right to give 42 days' notice and in other cases 90 days. Nevertheless, the landlord can sign a tenancy agreement relinquishing this right to give notice, say for a period of a year. However, the tenant still retains the right to give 21 days' notice. This has the effect of creating a "fixed-on-one-side-only" tenancy agreement. I have used this type of tenancy in the past to reassure a prospective and anxious tenant that mine is a long-term rental property. I do it by simply writing on the agreement a condition such as: "The landlord waivers his right to give notice to the tenant to terminate the tenancy, being notice with a termination date that falls within the period of 12 months beginning from the start date of this tenancy". This long sentence simply means that I can't give notice that has the effect of making the tenant leave within the first 12 months. However, it doesn't mean the tenant can stay there for 12 months and not pay the rent. All the tenant's normal responsibilities remain. The Tribunal can still terminate the tenancy for an unremedied breach or where rent is 21 days or more in arrears.

Discrimination

This is top of the list of "exemplary damages", carrying a maximum penalty of a $3000 fine. See p.64-65.

Rent

See chapter 6.

Bonds

Bond is defined in the Act (s.2) as "any sum of money payable or paid under a tenancy agreement as security for the observance and performance of the tenant's obligations under the agreement and this Act; but does not include any sum payable by way of rent."

All bond money collected by a landlord must be paid into the Bond Centre within 23 working days of receipt (see p.68). Alternatively, with the landlord's consent tenants themselves may pay the bond to the Centre. This is seldom to be recommended, as this way you lose control of the process.

If the tenant's bond cheque bounces, the tenant has failed one of their conditions of the tenancy agreement, by failing to pay bond. You therefore don't have to pay anything to the Bond Centre. You cannot, however, cancel the agreement for this reason. The best action you can take is to give the tenant a 10-day letter (see p.112). This is rather an unsatisfactory start to a tenancy and most likely an indication you have taken on a fraudster and a whole bag of trouble.

I am reluctant to accept a tenant's cheque for bond money — especially when renting at the bottom end of the market. I make it a condition of the tenancy that the bond be paid by cash, bank cheque or Social Welfare cheque.

The maximum bond you can require is the equivalent of 4 weeks' rent. However, the amount you will be able to collect in practice is likely to be less than this, owing to market conditions (see p.68-69). For tenants I am really dubious about I often ask for 4 weeks, at which point they typically give up pursuing the tenancy. However, there may in your town be no difficulty in collecting 4 weeks' worth. You need to have a feel for your market.

When receiving a bond you are required by the Act (s.19) to give a receipt showing the address of the tenancy, the amount of money and its nature (cash, cheque, etc.), the date and the name of the person paying it, if known.

After paying the bond to the Bond Centre, you will receive a bond refund form in the mail. If you wish to refund the bond in full to the tenant, only you need sign this form and send it back. If, however, some or all of the money is to come to the landlord, it is best if the form is signed by both parties. Sometimes, however, it can't be, e.g. when the tenant has abandoned the flat with rent in arrears. In this case, send the refund form in with only your signature on it. The Bond Centre has a procedure (s.22) of writing to the tenant and giving them 10 working days' notice of your claim to the bond. When postal service times and non-working days are added, you will need to wait at least 21 days (and probably a bit longer) for your money. If you send in your bank account number with the refund application form the money will be directly credited to your account. Otherwise they will send you a cheque in the mail.

If they do get a reply from the tenant disputing the payment to you, or perhaps the tenant complains about you on some other matter, your application is referred to your local Tenancy Services office and the mediation/tribunal process is swung into action to sort it out.

Landlord's obligations

Section 45 of the act is an easy one to read and understand. It lists the responsibilities a landlord has towards a tenant. Summarised briefly, they are as follows:

(a) At the start of the tenancy, give the premises to the tenant in a reasonable state of repair and cleanliness. (You are still bound by this obligation even if the tenant initially accepts the premises in a poor state.)

(b) Comply with all building, health and safety rules which apply to the building.

(c) Repay the tenant for reasonable expenses incurred in repairing the premises where the damage is the result of natural wear and tear and the tenant has made a reasonable attempt to give the landlord notice of the problem.

(d) Take all reasonable steps to ensure that other tenants don't interfere with the reasonable peace, comfort or privacy of the tenant. (See "quiet enjoyment" below)

(e) Except for normal repairs, a landlord may not cut off the water, electricity or gas to the premises. (In the past this was sometimes used to bring pressure to bear on tenants.)

As well as section 45 there are other obligations:

(f) The landlord is obliged to provide locks to ensure the premises are reasonably secure (s.46). This includes secure window catches as well as door locks. (The situation in New Zealand is not as onerous as in the United States where a jury awarded a woman tenant $17 million to be paid by the landlord. She had been raped by an intruder who gained easy access because the apartment block had poor quality locks.)

(g) The landlord is responsible for paying the rates, insurance and maintenance of the property (s.39(1)). The landlord can also agree to pay for other services such as power, gas, telephone, etc. This usually happens when the flat has not been separately set up with power and perhaps hot water (usually because it was built without a building consent!) However, these consumable supply charges are normally the tenant's responsibility.

When it comes to water, the tenant can be liable to pay for all the water they use if the following three conditions are met (s.39(2)): (i) the premises have a separate water meter. (ii) the tenancy agreement stated at the commencement of the tenancy, that the tenant shall pay for any metered water provided to the premises; and (iii) the water supplier charges for water provided to the premises on the basis of metered usage.

The water meter should be read at the start of a tenancy and the reading written on the tenancy agreement.

(h) When starting a tenancy, the landlord is obliged to give to the tenant his name, contact address, and address for service (s.15).
(i) The landlord is obliged to draw up a written tenancy agreement (s.13).
(j) The landlord must provide receipts for all money paid as bond (s.19) and all cash or negotiable cheques paid as rent (s.29).
(k) If the tenant asks for it in writing, the landlord must provide a written statement of the period to which any payment of rent relates (s.29). This means you need to have a record-keeping system that will, if required, produce a list of rents paid since the tenant moved in with a rent-paid-up-to date (s.30). (See p.107, 108.)
(l) If the landlord puts the property on the market he must immediately inform the tenant in writing, (s.47). When the property is sold the vendor is required to inform the tenant of the new owner (if known) and the changeover date (s.43).

Landlord's rights of entry

You can enter your property at any time that the tenant gives you an invitation to do so *immediately* before you enter (s.48). This means a tenant cannot be held to any agreement for you to enter at any time you like, no matter what they might have agreed to in the past. Without an invitation immediately before entry, your rights to enter are described in the Act, under this same section, and limited to:

(a) "In any case of emergency."
(b) Inspecting the premises, provided 48 hours' notice has been given within the last 14 days, specifying date and time of inspection. Such time to be between 8am and 7pm. You are not allowed to inspect the premises more than once every four weeks.
(c) For the purpose of checking that work has been done by the tenant to remedy a breach of his (for example, to check that the tenant has

fixed a hole in the wall you discovered in your last inspection). Once again, 48 hours' notice has to be given within the previous 14 days specifying date and time of inspection. Such time is to be between 8am and 7pm.

(d) For the purpose of carrying out repairs and maintenance, 24 hours' notice needs to be given and the notice needs to specify the reason for the entry. Such entry must be between 8am and 7pm.

(e) For the purpose of showing the premises to prospective tenants, prospective purchasers or a registered valuer, you may enter with the tenant's permission, and such permission "shall not be unreasonably withheld" but may be "subject to such reasonable conditions as the tenant may attach to the consent".

The Act does not require that notices to enter are to be written ones. However, I believe it is prudent to do so and **Appendix 6** (page 147), is a form that can be used for this.

Tenant's responsibilities

Section 40 lists most of the tenant's obligations. You do not need to list any of these as conditions on your tenancy agreement.

The tenant must:

(a) Pay the rent as and when it is due.

(b) Ensure the premises are occupied principally for residential purposes only.

(c) Keep the premises reasonably clean and reasonably tidy.

(d) Promptly notify the landlord of any damage to the property or any need for repairs.

(e) When leaving at the end of the tenancy, quit the premises, remove all goods and leave the place reasonably clean and reasonably tidy with the rubbish taken care of.

Also the tenant must *not* (s.40):

(f) Damage the property or permit others to damage it. (The next section, s.41 lays it on the line: the tenant is responsible for who goes and comes, and what visitors do while they are there. The tenant can use the Trespass Act to bar people whom they don't want. Often I tell tenants that they have this power and advise them to use it. Sometimes it all gets a bit vague, in a flatting situation, as to who is permitting whom to be on the premises.)

(g) Use the premises for any unlawful purpose.

(h) Cause or permit any interference with the reasonable peace, comfort or privacy of the landlord's other tenants or other neighbours.

(i) Fix any fixture to the premises or make alterations or renovations without the prior written consent of the landlord.

Also (s.40 (3)):

(j) Where the tenancy agreement limits the number of occupants the tenant must ensure this number is not exceeded. Often the word "occupant" can create some difficulties. It refers to permanent and not temporary visitors such as the auntie who visits for a couple of nights. However, a person who has no permanent abode at all may be legally taken to be residing at the place where they are temporarily staying. Therefore, strictly speaking, where there is a limiting-of-occupancy clause the tenant must not allow such drifters to stay even for one night. Such drifters typically account for 90% of the behavioural problems among your tenant's "guests".

(k) If damage occurs and the tenant says it was done by some third party (e.g. a totally unknown vandal) the landlord has only to prove the damage occurred during the time the tenant occupied the property. The onus is on the tenant to prove it wasn't him or one of his visitors that did it. (If the tenant is able to prove this then the landlord bears the cost.)

Also, under section 13A:

(l) When starting a tenancy, the tenant is required to enter into a written tenancy agreement giving the tenant's full name, address for service and contact address, and to tell the landlord if they are under the age of 18 years. (See p.71)

Tenants' quiet enjoyment

Tenants have rights to "quiet enjoyment and privacy" (s.38). If this is upset by the landlord or by other tenants, the Act has something to say about it. If you stick to the rules above about entering the premises and you don't disturb or deliberately infringe the tenant's privacy, you can generally enter the grounds of the property for a specific purpose, e.g. to do jobs in the grounds. If you are going to do more major work such as outside repainting, it is definitely advisable to make arrangements beforehand with the tenants.

Under the Act a tenant cannot bring an action against another tenant, but may complain to the landlord, who can act against the disruptive tenant. In fact the Act puts an obligation on the landlord to do so. As previously mentioned, in s.45 (1)(e), "The landlord shall...take all reasonable steps to ensure that none of the landlord's other tenants...[disturbs quiet enjoyment]."

In one case I took against a tenant with a noisy stereo, the Tribunal made a ruling for the tenant to abide by. Firstly, "no excessively loud music at any time," and secondly, "No music to be played after 10 pm or before 8am." Violation of one of these was sufficient grounds for another application to the Tribunal for termination. I photocopied the Tribunal's ruling, gave it to all the neighbours and said I wanted to be told of any violations. I didn't expect much to change, but in fact the neighbourhood did become relatively peaceful again.

Noisy people are also subject to the excessive-noise section of the Resource Management Act. These provisions are enforced by noise control officers of the local body. Acting on neighbours' complaints, the officers generally talk to offending parties and if that doesn't work they will serve a noise-abatement notice. They are even empowered to seize noise-making equipment.

The problem of noisy tenants in a block of flats annoying others goes with the territory. I did at one stage have the thought of running a block of flats just for noisy people. I would advertise, I thought, and fill it with people who liked playing loud music. However, I was wrong: even noisy neighbours like their neighbours to be quiet. For example, the ones that stay up late also sleep in late, and don't like being woken up in the mornings. In one extraordinary case, I had an unemployed couple leave a flat because they couldn't sleep through the sound of the schoolteacher blowing a whistle on the pedestrian crossing outside at 8.30 in the morning!

With more industry working night shifts there is increasing demand for a quiet daytime as well as night-time. The soundproofing of a block of flats is worth giving consideration to when buying or building. In a block of flats the party walls, which separate the units, don't have windows, and so often seem the logical place to put the stereo. Sometimes asking tenants to move the stereo to another wall will help, but ensure this doesn't simply create a new dispute with neighbours in a flat on the other side.

Apart from the construction of the buildings, the next best solution I have found is to have the neighbours talking to one another. Once I was getting complaints from one lot against another lot, who also had their own complaints against the first plus some more against a third lot of tenants — and so on. I invited them all to a meeting at which I shouted (sorry about the pun) a couple of dozen cans of beer. I introduced myself and each in turn introduced themselves. In the discussion that followed, they began talking to one another in a way that hadn't happened before. The conflicts between them began to be resolved — or at least I began to be left out of them. My thirty dollar "investment" in the beer as a means of tackling the problem, proved to be very worthwhile. Whenever I sign up a new tenant in a block of flats I now make a point of introducing them to as many of the others as possible.

Termination of tenancy

The Act deals at some length with the ending of tenancies — some 12 pages in fact. A tenancy can be ended by agreement, by notice of either party (after of course giving the required number of days' notice), or by a ruling of the Tenancy Tribunal. What is missing there is the ending of a tenancy for the reason that one party fails to perform. For example, if the tenant doesn't pay the rent and your patience has run out, you can't go in there and kick him or her out. The way you have to deal with a problem such as this, is by the mechanisms in the Act. That is a chain of actions that begin with an application to Tenancy Services, mediation (if it occurs) and then a tribunal decision. The Tribunal can order termination and award possession to you. The eviction, if necessary, can only be enforced by the bailiff of the court, who physically removes entrenched tenants. If necessary the bailiff will call on the police to assist with enforcing your rights.

Termination by notice

A notice to terminate must be in writing; it must identify the premises, specify the date the tenant is to vacate, and must be signed by the landlord (s.51). Probably no more than 10% of the notices to leave that tenants give me are in writing. However, if I am giving one I am always careful to put it in writing, and I strongly recommend that you do the same to avoid any argument over whether notice has been properly given. **Appendix 7** (p.148) is a suitable form for this purpose.

With periodic tenancies the tenant is required to give a minimum of 21 days, and the landlord to give a minimum of 90 days. This 90 days can be reduced to 42 days if the premises are required as a dwelling for the landlord, any member of his family, or one of his employees (if the property is owned for that purpose, and this fact is stated in the tenancy agreement), or if there is a signed and unconditional contract to sell the property on the basis of vacant possession. As with all notices, be aware of service times required (see p.98, 99).

When giving 42 days' notice you need to give the reasons for doing so. When giving 90 days' notice, however, you don't need to give any reasons. However, the Tribunal can declare any notice to terminate to be of no effect if it believes the motivation you had for giving the notice was in retaliation against the tenant's exercising any of their rights (s.54).

If you give a tenant notice and they want to leave before the date you specify in your notice, they are still bound by the 21 days. However, if they do leave earlier than that, and stop paying the rent, you are obliged to minimise your loss by taking whatever steps are reasonable under the circumstances to re-let the premises (s.49).

Grounds for termination by the Tribunal

There are four cases where you can make application to the Tribunal to end the tenancy. In the first three, the Tribunal *must* make an order terminating the tenancy if it is satisfied the facts of the case are true. These are:

1. The rent at the date on which you made the application to the Tribunal was at least 21 days in arrears. This is why you must always know the date to which the rent was paid up (see p.107, 108). However, the new

1996 amendment has introduced the concept of conditional termination orders in the case of rent arrears (s.55(1A & 1B). Now the tribunal can allow the tenant one last chance to pay off rent arrears on a set repayment schedule, but if this schedule is not adhered to, the order automatically takes effect as a final termination order.

2. The tenant has caused, permitted to be caused, or threatened, substantial damage to the premises.

3. The tenant has assaulted, or threatened to assault, the landlord (or his agents or members of his family) or any occupier or neighbour of the premises.

The Tribunal also *may* make an order if it is satisfied that:

(a) the tenant has committed a breach of the tenancy agreement or the act. If the breach is capable of remedy (almost all are) *and also*:

(b) The landlord gave the tenant a "10 working-day notice" (see p.112-114 for much more on 10-day letters) which with weekends and service time is practically 3 weeks. (In the case of rent in arrears this brings it close to the 21 days anyway) *and*:

(c) that the breach is of such a nature or of such an extent that it would be inequitable to refuse to end the tenancy.

Note: If an application is made for rent arrears under the 10-day letter provision it is likely that by the time the case comes to the Tribunal the tenant will be 21 days in arrears. In that case the Tribunal will consider the application as if it were a 21-days-in-arrears application, thus having stronger powers to order a termination (s.56(2).

Termination by agreement

Despite all the hassle-ridden endings of tenancies I have mentioned earlier, the most common way tenancies are ended is by agreement, and quite amicably. Typically the tenant rings up and gives notice (often less than 21 days); you advertise, get another replacement and it all changes over on the weekend by agreement of all parties. The outgoing tenant pays up to the start of the payments of the incoming one, and despite all the comings and goings you hope that the place is left clean and tidy between tenancies. (Better still, check this, as you have an obligation to do so.) (See p.89.) It is so much easier when things are done by agreement.

Abandonment of premises

Abandonment of premises is not defined in the Act. In practice there is a range of behaviour that may go under the heading of abandonment. One scenario may be that the "flat" is getting behind with the rent, you began hassling them about this, one or two flatmates leave, then it appears that the last one has left — but nobody has handed in a key or cleaned up and you cannot be sure what the situation is. Of course, the rent hasn't been paid for at least a couple of weeks by now. Given that written notices from this class of tenant are rare, what are you supposed to do? Well, what I do is clean up, maybe change locks, advertise and re-let. Then I make a one-party claim for the bond and leave it at that. The Act, however, seems to suggest you need first to make an application to the tribunal for possession of premises.

The absconding tenant is liable to pay rent for 21 days from the date the landlord "became aware, or ought to have reasonably become aware" that the tenant had abandoned the premises, or from that date up to the date of the start of a new tenancy. It's your problem to try and get it from them though, and that can be difficult to say the least; plus a week or two of delay for a tribunal hearing only adds further to the liability. That is why I am likely to act on my own.

Another scenario is where the rent is not paid and you go to the flat and the tenant's possessions are there — but you can never find the tenant there. Also, the neighbours haven't seen him either. It would be advisable to take an application to the tribunal for abandonment of premises in this case.

Abandoned goods

This issue is covered under section 62 of the Act. Sometimes on the termination of a tenancy or in the abandonment of a tenancy, things are left behind — both valuable and worthless. Under the Act, rubbish can be taken to the dump and perishable foodstuffs anywhere you want; but the rest is the problem: goods, valuable or otherwise. If there is a house lot of valuables then it is best to comply with the Act, to the letter. Often, however, there are only one or two items of furniture of dubious value. It has been left because it was not needed at the new flat the tenant went to, and their friends don't want it. Perhaps it came from a charitable furniture bank (if I know this I give it back.)

I have a big basement and I put the stuff there. It usually gets loaned out to other incoming tenants, with the provision, "If the original people want it back I will have to get it back from you." I have only had to do this once — the owner wasn't a tenant of mine but had his stuff stored in a garage at my flat. When the tenant left, he left the stuff behind, not even knowing the owner's full name or where he was. It turned out the owner was in jail and when he got out he looked me up. It was about 18 months later by this time, and most of the stuff had long gone out of my basement. However, I negotiated a deal whereby I gave him a selection of other stuff that was in there, and he was able to set up his new place reasonably well. It could have ended up worse for me, and I have a less cavalier attitude towards other people's stuff nowadays.

The requirement (s.62(b)) is to secure the goods in safe storage and "forthwith" to apply to the tribunal for an order for the disposal of the goods. The tribunal may order the goods to be returned to the tenant (if it is known where they are), or that they be sold. From the money gained in their sale, the tribunal may award you the cost of storing and dealing with the goods, and also any other money the tenant may owe you. Other than this, any profit from their sale goes to the Ministry of Housing. The tenant may apply at any time up to a year later to claim this money.

In this whole business the tenant is in breach of s.40(1)(e): "The tenant shall...on termination of the tenancy...remove all his or her goods from the premises." There are no exemplary damages available against the tenant — only compensation for actual and reasonable costs in dealing with the goods.

Serving notice (s.136)

Working under the Act you will find you are serving notices a lot. For example, a 42-day notice to leave, a 10-day warning letter to "remove the dog from the premises," or the common one: "pay the rent in advance as per our tenancy agreement." When you give the tenant such a letter, they may later say, "But I didn't get that letter". However, if you give the letter in any of the ways set down in the Act, "it is sufficient" and the tenant is "deemed" to have received the letter and therefore has no comeback. The ways are as follows:

1. Go to the property and give it to the tenant, or anyone who lives there and who looks at least 16 years old.
2. Leave it in the mailbox or attached to the door in a prominent position.
3. Post it to the tenant at the tenant's address for service (note that this may not be the address of the rental premises — see below).
4. Give it to the person who normally pays the rent on the property.

5. Give it to the tenant's solicitor or other authorised agent of the tenant.
6. Fax it to a number specified in the tenancy agreement.
7. Deliver it to the place of residence of the tenant (where this is different from the tenancy address).

In these notices you often give a date after which you will take some specific action, e.g. a 48-hours notice of inspection. In calculating this date you need to allow some additional days for delivery of the letter (s.136 (6&7)). If you post the letter, you have to allow 4 working days for its delivery. If you take the letter to the premises and tack it on the door or leave it in the letterbox, allow 2 working days. This means, for example, if you are posting a 10-day letter you must allow 10 *working* days to start with, *plus* the weekends (and any statutory holidays) *plus another 4 working days* after it was posted.

If, however, you give the notice directly to a proper person (such as the tenant, one of his agents, or any of the others listed above) you don't need to allow any such extra time.

Address for service

When you are signing up a tenancy agreement, as already discussed in chapter 4, make sure you have an address for service for the tenancy. Section 16 of the Act obliges the tenant to provide the landlord with an address for service, which is "the address at which notices and other documents relating to the tenancy will be accepted by or on behalf of the tenant." Normally this is the address of the property you are renting out, but often it is useful to make it some other more permanent address, for example with a flat of students you might use their parents' address. This can be helpful when the tenancy is over and you are chasing the tenant for a bond refund or damages, etc.

Enforcing tribunal orders

Most tribunal orders against tenants either order them to pay you money or to give you possession of the premises.

Orders for possession. The court bailiff can physically remove tenants under a tribunal order. The bailiff can call on the police to assist. Surprisingly perhaps, physical eviction seldom seems to be necessary and I don't have any personal experience of it.

Money orders. More usually you will have a tribunal order, say, ordering the tenant to pay you $550 by a date that was last Wednesday, and they haven't paid a dollar. They are no longer one of your tenants and you don't know where they are now living. Perhaps you are new in the business of residential rentals and are shocked by this flagrant disregard of the orders of the "most high" tribunal. Well, all I can say is "welcome". This is rather the usual situation with money orders from the tribunal. What can be done?

Firstly, if you haven't got a new address for them you will find it hard even to get started. Each circumstance varies. It is much harder if they have left town. It is easier in a small town than a big city to find out where somebody lives. Maybe the neighbours know. Maybe you can get their number from Directory Service, ring them and ask their new address. Maybe you can find out where they are living by contacting an employer. (The Income Support Service is no help. They will pass on letters but can't, under the Official Information Act, disclose addresses.) Perhaps you have the phone number or address of their parents — or they may have a relatively unusual surname and you can try tracing them through the phone book. Perhaps your local power supply office will know and tell you where they are now using power. You may try ringing all the "to-let" adverts describing their type of accommodation advertised the day or so before they suddenly left. Ask these advertising landlords if they have rented to your absconding tenants. I generally find that with methods such as these I can trace somebody who stays in my small town, but if they leave town my chances diminish. If I lose them I may give the tenancy order to Baycorp, the national debt-collecting agency. Given a few months or a few years, these people have a habit of turning up on Baycorp's computer over another matter, and then something can be done about mine.

If you have got an address, there are two courses of action. Firstly, you can hand the tribunal order over to a debt-collection firm anyway. They typically will attempt to get the money by contacting the tenants first, and when this fails the debt collectors will go through the legal processes for you. First they will usually want about $100 up front from you. This is often recoverable from the debtor if they are successful, but there is of course no guarantee of this.

Secondly, you can pursue the matter yourself through the Justice Department. To do so, you front up to the courthouse, show them your tribunal order and fill in a form. Along with the form you will be asked to pay a "filing fee" of $50-120 (depending on which course of action is to be taken as described below). The fees you pay can be added on to what the debtor owes you (but of course, as also can be the case with using debt collectors, you might also be throwing good money after bad). If you are a serious do-it-yourself landlord, use the excellent workbook by the lawyer Scotney Williams (see Appendix 1).

A tribunal order is enforceable as an order (judgment) of the District Court, and as such the Registrar of the Court and the bailiffs of the Court have a number of remedies for delinquent "judgment debtors". These remedies are:

Warrant of Distress. This is a system whereby the bailiff goes to the debtor's house and takes things of value to sell. Tools of trade up to a maximum value of $500, or necessary wearing apparel and household furniture to a maximum value of $2000, are protected from such seizures. Goods that are seized must be sold by public auction, and from the proceeds you can be paid. Usually the goods are redeemed by their owners fronting up with the money shortly after seizure. This system works when the debtor has something of decent resale value. However, many problem debtors don't, or will claim their valuables aren't really their own but belong to someone else.

Garnishee proceedings. This is where money or assets held by a third party are accessed by the court — by use of a "charging order". For example, money in a bank account, company shares that can be sold, or income from a trust. Charging orders are not common in our business for the same reasons as distress warrants — there may be no known assets.

Order for examination. This is the necessary preliminary to obtaining an "attachment order" (see below). Examinations are conducted by the court and must take place in the presence of the judgment debtor.

When you apply for an examination, you need to pay some money over to the court to be given to the debtor! This is called "conduct money". This money is for the judgment debtor to pay for the most economical public transport to and from the court. Usually it only need be a few dollars. I once tracked one of my absconding tenants down and found they now lived across the road from the court house — no more than 200 meters away from the front door of the court. I still paid $1 which was duly given to her by the court official. She still failed to appear and so the court was able to move onto the next step which was to arrest her, walk her to court and do the examination.

At the examination the judgment debtor's income, expenditure, assets and liabilities are examined. Then an amount is set that is judged they can afford to pay weekly from their income and this can be collected by an "attachment order". This is an order of the court to the employer of the judgment debtor. It orders the employer to deduct from the income of the debtor specified sums of money for a specified time. Benefits from the social welfare department and A.C.C. payments can have attachment orders placed on them. Sometimes the debtor's debts are large and their income small so that the amount you get per month is only a few dollars, — and perhaps they owe you hundreds of dollars.

Sorry, them's the breaks. As I told you, prevention is better than cure. You cannot get blood out of a stone. That is the end of this chapter and the end of the cliches!

Chapter 6

Collecting the rent

Rent is the lifeblood of your business. It pays your bills and if the bills are not paid your business will fail. Most tenants realise this, but some don't. They think it is all disposable income for you — perhaps it is. Whatever the attitude of your tenants, it doesn't matter: rent has to be paid and you need to ensure it is paid — and paid on time. This chapter is about developing a rent collection policy.

Setting the rent

You don't set the rent: the market does, so you need to have a feel for this. It can be difficult keeping up with the market, especially if you only have one or two properties. The best way is probably to study the to-let column in the newspaper. Also, you can ask other rental-property owners, or perhaps contact a rental-property manager and ask about current rents. A rent set below market levels will create a greater response to your advertisement and so give you a greater choice in tenant selection. Lower rents are also likely to lead to tenants staying longer — less turnover and so less work for you. It won't, however, influence tenant behaviour in the property. Tenants are unlikely to take any more care of the property because it is cheaper. Likewise, if they are unreliable about paying their rent, they are usually just as unreliable about a paying a lower rent as a higher one.

On the other hand, rents set above the market level are a sure-fire way to increase the work you will need to put into the property. High turnover and a poor choice of tenants are the usual outcomes.

One of the more difficult periods for you will be when and if rent levels fall in your market. You are likely first to notice this happening when you have a vacancy and a poor response to an advertisement. If you have a block of flats, for example, do you first drop the rent on just the vacant one to get a tenant, or do you lower the rent on all the others as well, to be fair? I don't have any expert answer to this. Personally, I am quick enough to lower the rent on the vacant one but will only lower the rents on the others if I believe my good tenants are otherwise likely to leave. In my experience, tenants seldom talk amongst themselves about their rents and so it is relatively easy to have varying rents for the same flats. The management of a block of flats is a business where deals are done between individuals, and one flat may well be rented at a lower price than another.

Collection methods

There are many ways to physically get the rent from tenants. The best is the way that works best for both you and the tenant. In some cases you may need to use the method of payment as a selection criterion, i.e. select a tenant in the first place who can pay the rent in the manner you need it to be paid. There are four common methods of rent collection:

Personal payment

With many tenants, the best way to collect the rent is a personal, and regular visit, either of them to you or you to them. Perhaps you run a business in town where they can call and pay you, or you live on or near the premises and they can visit. Or you can go and collect the rent from the flat yourself. The advantage of this personal approach is that you regularly meet the tenant and, if you visit them, you can keep an eye on the flat. Under section 29 of the Act you are required to "forthwith" give a receipt for cash received as rent. The receipt must show the address of the premises (or a code), the amount of money, the date, and the name of the person paying the money (if known).

The most common system of receipting this money is to use a rent book. These are sold by bookshops or stationers. The book is kept by the tenant, who presents it together with the money on rent day. You fill it out, sign it and take the money.

Superior though it is, I have never been in a position to offer this method of payment. It requires you to be available on every rent day to receipt the rent. Particularly at the bottom end of the market, I don't want my tenants to have to keep their rent in cash waiting for me to appear when I can't make it on rent day — they or somebody else are likely to spend it.

Automatic payment

This is the most favoured way, from my point of view. A set amount of money regularly passes from the tenant's bank account to yours. When the money comes into my bank account there is plenty of information on my statement as to where the money came from.

Automatic payments are, however, no guarantee that the rent will be paid. If there is insufficient funds to cover the whole amount — even just 50 cents short — nothing gets paid to you. Furthermore, with some inter-bank transfers, if there was not enough money in the tenant's bank account in the first place, the transaction may go through, only to be reversed a day or two later — usually after you have ticked the rent off as paid! It takes a bit of the shine off the system when this happens.

Automatic payments may never work for some tenants. Your tenant may never have sufficient funds in their account, but they can pay the rent by collecting first each portion from their flatmates, so they end up with a bundle of cash, which needs to get into your bank account as soon as possible. This brings us to the next method of payment.

Cash deposit to your bank account

This is where the tenant fronts up to your bank and deposits direct to your account. If you have more than one property, ask your bank what they can offer you to make this method work best, as the various banks are able to offer a range of systems of marking who has been depositing what.

If you can, give your tenant at least a pre-numbered deposit book with a space for teller stamps. The tenant ends up with a rubber stamp from the bank as a receipt of money paid, and the money goes automatically to the correct account.

The one problem I have had with this system is the lack of any indication on my bank statement as to where the money came from. This is particularly a problem where I have, for example, a block of flats all at $135 a week — if one tenant doesn't pay, how do I know which one? Also, sometimes, a tenant may be a bit short, or a bit flush, and pay more or less than the normal rent. So there is an odd amount sitting there — who paid it?

Well there are two solutions I have found. The first is to never have two rents the same. Once I bought a couple of flats, both of them at $105 a week rent, and I already had an existing flat on that rent. I re-negotiated the rent on one of the new flats to $104.90 and on the other to $104.95. Then I could always be sure who had paid what. Normally, though, I have at a least a 50-cent difference. I also like having "hard" numbers. $117.50 rent a week is a hard number while $120 is a soft number — it is as though $117.50 is the true calculated rent for that property; it is a psychological thing.

The second solution is to use an individual numbering system available from your bank. What each bank has to offer and what it costs varies. You need to make some enquires yourself. Some banks have more advanced electronic data processing than others and so can offer more options. In my experience all banks have got pleasant, smiling staff — but some have better computers than others.

A cheque in the mail

Payment by cheque is almost universal in North America, where rents are paid monthly, but it is uncommon in New Zealand. Here, you will be dealing with smaller, more regular amounts of money and the delay of the mail and then the cheque bouncing can all mean you are a week or more behind with an unscrupulous tenant. But once again, if it suits the tenant, and you have a good tenant, and it suits you, what's wrong with it? You may want to give the tenants a supply of stamped self-addressed envelopes to help them post it regularly.

Note that under the Act (s.29), non-negotiable cheques do not need to be receipted. Also, under s.23(3) you cannot require a tenant to give you a series of post-dated cheques.

The Tenancy Act and rent

Rent is defined in the Act as "any money, goods, service or other valuable consideration."

You are not allowed to "require" the payment of any rent more than 2 weeks in advance, or, the payment of rent before the expiry of the period for which rent has been paid already. This eliminates two forms of rental payment methods:

Monthly rent. Rent 12 times a year is out. There is nothing to stop a tenant paying it this way, or you receiving it, but don't go writing a tenancy agreement with it in because you are starting to "require" something that is illegal.

If the tenant does pay monthly rent but one month is not paid, you are on your own trying to get a whole month's rent in advance out of them: the Tribunal won't enforce this for you. In fact, on application by the tenant you may have awarded against you $750 in "exemplary damages" (s.109(c)). *Rent always in advance.* The frustrating thing for rental-property owners receiving rent in advance is that once rent day comes it is no longer rent in advance. It has all been used up. Take the case of the tenant who moves in to the flat on Thursday 1 November and pays 2 weeks' rent in advance. The tenant lives there day by day until the 15th, when rent is due again. If the tenant fails to pay on the 15th they immediately slip into arrears, compounding as each day goes by. To solve this problem, many owners used a scheme where the tenant pays two weeks rent on the day of moving in and then two weeks rent again a week later, with the third lot of rent a fortnight later to start the regular fortnightly pattern. This way the tenant is always at least a week in advance. This system was common in many parts of New Zealand. It is really a system of having a week's bond in hand "rolling along" as it were. For this reason it has been outlawed by the Act because the government wants all bond paid into its coffers. To back this up, there is available to the tribunal a $750 exemplary damages penalty against landlords who collect rent this way (s.109(4c)).

Calculating daily rent

Although you may be charging rent on a weekly or fortnightly basis, under the Tenancy Act rent accrues on a daily basis. You need to be able to calculate this. The way I figure it, rent accrues on a nightly basis. If it is Thursday 1 November and the tenant moves into the flat and stays there the night, one day's rent is due. If you count 14 nights from, and including the 1st, you are up to the night of the 14th and rent is due on the 15th in order to pay for that night. If they stay 6 months and move out on a Thursday, any incoming tenant can pay for Thursday night, but the outgoing tenant gets Thursday free because they are not there that night. You could think of it this way: the days are free but the nights you pay for — sound familiar?

You always need to have a clear idea of the date *to which* rent has been paid. This is important if tenants pay rent in bits and pieces. If they don't pay the rent in full you need to be able to work out the date up to which it has been paid. The formula is the same as working out the first part-payment of a new tenancy. Simply work out how much rent per night you are charging (by dividing the weekly rent by 7) and then divide this figure into the part payment you have received. For example:

$135 weekly rent paid only by $100
$135 divided by 7 = $19.28 per day
$100 divided by $19.28 = 5.18 days rent paid. Round down to five days.

When setting rents consider the advantage of having weekly rents set at a multiple of 7 (the days in a week). For example $119, which is 17 multiplied by 7, $126 which is 18 multiplied by 7, and so on. It makes the arithmetic easier.

Rent increases

In times of high inflation, the business of increasing the rent is an ongoing one. With low inflation, it is more common only to review rent levels at a change of tenants.

The basic rule in the Act (s.24) is that you cannot increase the rent within 180 days (six months) of the start of the tenancy, or within 180 days of any previous increase. Also, you can only increase the rent after having given to the tenant 60 days' notice in writing.

Prompt-payment policies

Most tenants pay rent as regularly as the calendar counts the weeks. Probably about 80% are like this. The other 20% are not, and they cause 80% of the work.

In my business, rent day is Thursday and check-up-on-rent-day is Friday. Any tenants who are late with their rent payment can expect to receive a phone call if they are on the phone, or a visit or letter if they are not, either on the Friday or during the weekend.

With a few notable exceptions, it is not often that I have tenants vacate a property while still owning me rent, or owing me rent beyond the level of their bond. A policy of closely monitoring rent payments and holding a bond gets me paid up in almost all cases.

The Act outlaws any system of financial incentives or penalties for prompt rental payments. A discount if the rent is paid on time, or a late fee if rent is paid late, is illegal under section 32. The banks may charge you penalty interest if you are late with your mortgage payments, but you cannot charge your tenants a similar penalty.

Communication

In dealing with rent arrears, effective communication is important. Every tenant is an individual and it is worth trying to understand how it is best to approach each.

For example, one middle-aged woman tenant lived in a property I managed. I was working at a real estate firm at the time and she paid her rent by a cheque over the counter. She paid on the days she came to town — not following a regular routine. In doing so she had dropped a week's rent behind. To make matters worse, the office staff when receipting the money had made a mistake with the date-paid-to dates they wrote on her recipts and showed her as being up-to-date when she wasn't. This had happened a couple of months before and I hadn't picked it up until now. She had an up-market rental which was kept immaculate. I knew she would be touchy to approach. I thought if I rang her I would have some difficulty describing this problem simply, being as it was one of dates and details. I wrote to her what I thought was a gentle and polite letter showing the dates and amounts paid, etc. Well, the tone of my letter must have been just half an octave out of tune as she took great offence. I had to talk to her to apologise for everything all over again — including my letter. She paid the rent arrears, no problem there. It was only my style of communication that was at fault.

At the other end of the scale, I can easily recall tenants for whom strongly worded legal-type letters seem to have about as much effect as hailstones on an army tank. One family of recent immigrants from the Pacific Islands seemed immune to my letters and phone calls. What I learnt to do was to visit, talk only to the man of the household, and do so as if we were two diplomats: lots of small talk before the business and careful throughout to respect his pride and his position as head of the household. Communication then was effective. This is a time-consuming method. On the other hand, Tenancy Service mediation and tribunal hearings are even more so.

Managing rent arrears

When tenants get behind with their rent, you may not realistically be able to get up to date with one lump sum as the tenant struggles with all the other demands on their cash. Nevertheless, you as the provider of shelter from the weather have first priority. For example, the rankings of a budget advisor are likely to look like this:

1. Current rent/mortgage
2. Electricity
3. Food
4. Telephone
9. Schools
5. Car payments
6. Insurance
7. Taxes
8. Heating fuel
9. Doctors
10. Dentists
11. New clothing
12. Club dues

Note that current rent is right at the top.

The attitude to take with tenants in default is to be firm, fair and fast. Of these three, the last is the most important. I am also firm. I am in business and I always mean business when collecting rents. Fair, the third of the three, means to me, acting in a rational rather than a emotional way.

Many rental-property owners are busy people, managing their one or three rental properties on a part-time basis. It is easy for them to "discover" that flat one hasn't paid rent for the last month. They are then faced with attempting to collect large sums of money from people who never have more than a week's worth of spending money in their bank at any one time — and that's only there on the day they get it.

You and I are probably similar when it comes to money. We own property so we know something about the difference between capital and cash flow: something about having money and not needing to spend it. Other people are not the same: they spend all the money they get whenever they get it. If for some reason they keep my rent instead of paying it to me, it won't last a week. It goes like early morning mist.

I recall a young couple with two babies living in one of my flats under the protection of a budget adviser/controller who paid me the rent. I was there once and the woman was in an agitated state because her man had the task of walking home with $200 cash — a huge windfall for them. His path would take him through town. He was under strict instructions to deliver the cash safely home, but nevertheless her fears were well-founded. He arrived home, from memory, with a CB two-way radio and no money.

The qualities of successful rent collectors are persistence, consistency and timeliness. The most important is timeliness.

When I was a part-time landlord, I still kept up to date with rental payments. Rents were due on Thursdays, my bank posted me a Friday bank statement, and this was delivered to my home on Saturday. I was only 2 days behind the play and it worked well.

The best value-for-money service available to landlords is that provided by banks. The bank is open regular hours and can act as a cashier receiving payments from our clients. It supplies a printout on demand (perhaps even with a 24-hour lobby machine facility), or gives an up-to-date balance when telephoned to check up on a payment. However, the bank is only the bookkeeper. You need to be the manager of your rent collection. To do this you need a rent-collection policy and an effective structure to implement that. Here are three suggested steps you may consider when developing a rent-collection policy for defaulting tenants.

Contact the tenant and listen to their explanation. This is easier if they are on the phone or can be rung at work. A tenant on automatic payment may not know the rent hasn't been paid. One common glitch is where the tenant leaves enough money in their account for the auto-payment, but the bank takes out its fee first and now they are a few cents short of the full amount — so no payment at all is made.

After a while you begin to know what to expect from each tenant. Some with a history of late payment become adept at blaming others. A common excuse is to blame the bank, but in my experience it is extremely rare for banks to make mistakes.

Follow up the tenant's promises. On this initial contact, the tenant will usually give a reason and then offer a promise. For example, "I didn't get paid yesterday because the computer at work failed. The money should be there on Wednesday so I can pay the rent then." I respond, "So you will pay two lots of rent on Thursday, which is $260 total?" "Yes," says the tenant. Depending on how I "read" the tenant, however, I may follow up a conversation such as this with a letter: "This letter is to confirm our conversation of [date]. You are in arrears of rent. You agreed that on Thursday 14 June you will pay a total of $260 to bring you up to date." A stronger approach would be to add to this letter a 10-day notice as well.

Ten-day notice letter

There are two grounds upon which the tribunal may order termination of tenancy because of rent arrears:

1. When the tenant has failed to remedy the breach of rent arrears after having been given 10 days notice to do so (s.56).
2. Where rent is more than 21 days in arrears (s.55).

See the sample 10-day letter (**Figure 1.**) A blank copy of this is supplied in this book as **Appendix 8** on p.149. The 10 days you need to give a tenant to fix things up are 10 *working* days, which allowing for weekends will always mean 14 days, and with public holidays and service times (see p.98, 99), even longer.

The 10-day letters as per s.56 is a general letter for use by either party for any breach by the other party of the Act or tenancy agreement. For example, you can send one for the presence of a dog on the property when the tenancy agreement prohibits dogs, or excessive noise, obstructing driveways and so on.

When using a 10-day letter for rent arrears, if the tenant continues to pay no rent for the next few weeks, the 10-day letter becomes irrelevant, as the 10 working days in reality is more like 21 calendar days, and 21

To: Mr Jeremiah Tenant
Flat 1
63 View Street
Morristown

10 DAY NOTICE TO REMEDY
(PURSUANT TO S(56) OF THE RESIDENTIAL TENANCIES ACT 1986)

I Frank Saxton acting as landlord hereby give you 10 working days notice to remedy the breach of the tenancy agreement/~~provisions of the act~~ (delete one) as set out below:

Our tenancy agreement provides for rent to be paid weekly in advance. The rent due last Thursday 1st November was not paid. Your rent is paid only to 30 October and is now in arrears.

Please remedy this breach of our tenancy agreement.

TAKE NOTICE THAT IF YOU FAIL OR REFUSE to remedy the breach within the time specified the landlord will be entitled to apply to the Tenancy Tribunal for an order terminating the tenancy.

Signed

Landlord — 11/2/94 Date

Figure 1: A sample 10-day letter (See p.112).

days in arrears is the big gun (see p.114). Still, the 10-day letter has two uses. Firstly, it is a legal letter and signals to the tenant that you are serious. Secondly, if the tenant pays some rent within the 10 days (and so gets a bit safer from being close to or over 21 days in arrears), but does not pay all the rent owing, you are in a position to take some legal action that you could not otherwise.

Just because a 10-day letter has been issued, doesn't mean all communication between you and the tenant must cease. Phone calls, occasional visits and follow-ups on promises made along the way are all methods of keeping the communication going and prompting action. However, in your

communication with the tenant I suggest you don't compromise the 10-day letter. Leave it standing with its days ticking over. Furthermore, whenever you are in dispute with a tenant (such as rent arrears) you can apply to the tribunal for a remedy to the dispute. In other words, you can go to mediation and if need be on to the tribunal to seek redress — it is just that without any 10-day period having run its course the tribunal can't order termination of the tenancy.

At the end of the 10 days it may be that some rent has been paid since the letter was issued, but not enough for the tenant to be fully up to date. You have the option now that if an application for termination is made to the tribunal it can terminate the tenancy if it so chooses.

An application for termination where rent is 21 days in arrears

The rule here is that the rent must be more than 21 days in arrears on the day you lodge with the tribunal an application form asking for termination.

The 21 days must be a 21 days' difference between the paid-to date and the date of application. Take the case for example of a tenant who is required to pay fortnightly rent in advance, and rent day is Thursday 1 November. If rent is not paid and today is 2 November the tenant is a day's rent in arrears — not the 14 days' worth of rent you were counting on to be in your bank account. You have to wait until 22 November (and receive no rent in the meantime) before the tenant will be 21 days in arrears. Also, while you are waiting for 21 days to come up, the tenant may pay some rent, and perhaps keep paying enough rent to never get 21 days behind, but always be in arrears. This is where the 10 day letter, as discussed above, is most useful.

Chapter 7

Record keeping and taxation

In chapter 1 we discussed the need for professional advice before purchasing a property. Now that you have bought the property, you should get some advice from an accountant about the record keeping necessary for your business. Record keeping presents a choice: either the accountant will do all the book work, or you will do it with their advice.

The bookwork for the business of one or a few rental units is a simple task. I suggest you do it yourself and, after the initial setting-up discussion, and perhaps the odd phone call during the year for advice, in a normal year only visit your accountant once. Make this visit at the time that your tax return is completed but before it is sent to the IRD. At this visit your work can be checked over and some further advice received about the forthcoming year.

There are two purposes for keeping records. One is to satisfy the requirements of the Inland Revenue Dept for tax calculation, and the second is to provide information for better management. I will describe a simple single-entry bookkeeping system suitable for tax calculation (subject to your accountant's advice) for the new owner with one rental property. (This property may be a block of flats, but it is still one property.) Following this is some advice about bookkeeping if you own more than one property.

For many owners it is an annual headache to produce a tax return. A couple of years ago a friend of mine who owned a simple block of 5 units was 18 months late with his returns. The task seemed so daunting to him, he had difficulty even starting the job and every day found another excuse not to do so. There is no need for it to be like this. Following a few simple rules and keeping the book-work up to date it is (almost) a pleasure.

A note about GST. Residential rental property is exempt from GST. This means you do not charge GST on your rents and, even if you are registered, you cannot claim GST on any of the expenses incurred in your residential rental business.

Making a loss? Remember the "business test"

If you are running your rental at a profit, the IRD will happily agree with you that you have a business and accept the tax you pay from the profit. If, however, you run it at a loss, you need to satisfy the requirements of the business test. These are: that you are in this activity for the purpose of making a profit, and that you have the intention of making a profit and the reasonable prospect of doing so. Throughout this chapter I will make some reference to what you can do to go towards meeting these requirements.

Accounting for one rental property

Bank account for keeping the money in

As discussed in chapter 6, you need a separate cheque account solely for your new rental business. This helps satisfy the business test, as it reinforces purpose and intention to run it as a business — not, for example, to provide accommodation for members of your family. Into this bank account will go all your rents and out of it will come all the expenses. If your rental is negatively geared you will probably need to deposit some of your own money into it from time to time, to keep it going. On the other hand, if it is making a profit you can withdraw funds — perhaps on a regular basis.

Files for keeping all those documents in

What filing system are you going to use? I suggest three ring binder folders (and a two-hole punch). Into the first folder will go all copies of the title, valuation reports, mortgage documents, insurance premiums and so on. If you have dividers with these various labels on them the records are more easily kept orderly.

The second folder is for tenant records. It is divided up by flat address: flats 1, 2, 3, etc. Into each division will go copies of tenancy agreements,

correspondence to tenants and tenancy bond centre documentation. When you are going off to see a tenant you can grab the tenant folder and have all the records you need. In this folder I also put some sheets of blank paper, envelopes and carbon paper. With these resources in my tenant folder I have the ability to leave notes for people who are not at home — and also put down in writing on the spot agreements regarding repairs, payment of late rent, etc. Every couple of years I go through my tenant folder and remove from it all documents from expired tenancies and put these in storage. This way the folder is kept lean and current.

The third folder is for keeping bank statements. I get one statement a week from my rental account — so that is 52 statements a year and they are all there in order. As well as the bank statements, there are mortgage account statements. These come perhaps once every 3 or 6 months. They may also be accommodated in the rear of this third folder.

At the end of the financial year, all statements are bundled up (along with all expense receipts for the year) and put into a big envelope for long-term storage.

Money in — rents received

You are likely to receive rents in three different ways from tenants: as cash (or cheque) direct from them; by the tenant making a deposit over the counter at your bank, or by automatic bank transfer. The money you receive direct from the tenants leaves you with the task of depositing it into the bank account while with the other two ways it is done for you. Arrange for a weekly statement from your bank. As discussed in chapter 4, by having all your tenants pay on Thursdays you can make Fridays the rent-checking-up-on day. This checking off is done into a rent book.

Figure 2 is an example of a rent book. Each horizontal line represents a week on which rent is due. The date due is a column of Thursdays. In this example flat 1 has paid regularly every week on due date. Flat 2 has been running late and in fact this tenant is two payments behind schedule. Flat 3 pays every fortnight and a simple line alternatively cancels out the alternative weeks when no money is due. Flat 4 show an example of a tenancy changeover where an outgoing tenant paid $48 for three days while the incoming tenant paid $64 for 4 days' rent, making $112 for the full week. There are 40 horizontal lines in my rent book. I use 26 lines for the first 6 months of the year and another page for the other 6 months. The columns

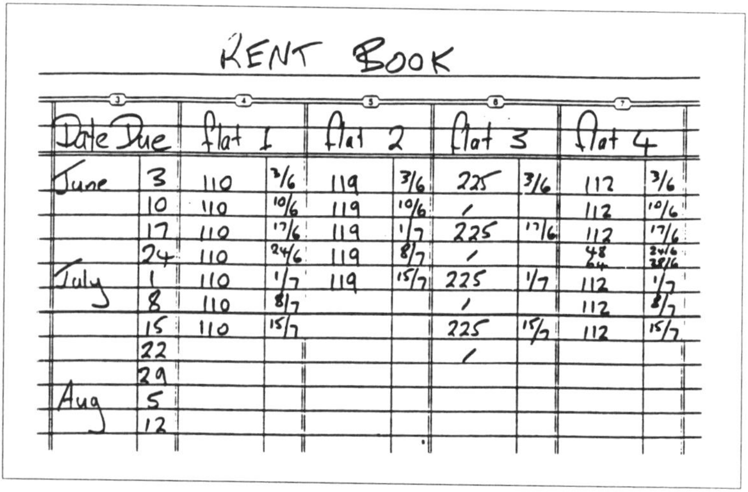

RENT BOOK

Date Due		Flat 1		Flat 2		Flat 3		Flat 4	
June	3	110	3/6	119	3/6	225	3/6	112	3/6
	10	110	10/6	119	10/6	/		112	10/6
	17	110	17/6	119	1/7	225	17/6	112	17/6
	24	110	24/6	119	8/7	/		48 64	24/6 28/6
July	1	110	1/7	119	15/7	225	1/7	112	1/7
	8	110	8/7			/		112	8/7
	15	110	15/7			225	15/7	112	15/7
	22					/			
	29								
Aug	5								
	12								

Figure 2: A sample rent book page.

in each page are added up at the end of the year to give me a figure for annual rents received.

Besides rent, you will also receive bond money from tenants. It is important to keep this separate from rents, as it is not income and you don't want to be paying income tax on it. Have a separate column for bond. One column is usually enough for all the flats involved. Write on your bank statement and again next to the entry in the rent book, a note saying from which tenancy the money has come.

Money out — expenses

The exact definition of expenses and capital, and the difference between them, is subject to a highly complex body of law that helps to keep numerous accountants and lawyers in business. Unfortunately all that is beyond the scope of this book. However, recent court cases have shifted things so the matter now turns on "change to market value". Take the example of repainting the inside of a flat: maybe there is a wooden window that has rotted in one corner, so you get a good second-hand one and put it in. Overall, this is standard maintenance and the market value of the property is pretty well unchanged — so the cost is a maintenance expense. However, it is a capital expense if you do something that significantly increases the market value of the property, e.g. adding a new garage or building on another room. That will lift the price you could expect to sell the house for, so it is regarded as a capital expense.

But what if you are making renovations that involve both run-of-the-mill repairs and some more general improvements that will lift the market value? The answer is to make some split of the money spent into repairs and capital. Each case is different and the advice of your accountant will be invaluable. If you are going to spend a significant amount of money on a property, get your accountant's advice on the taxation effects before you do so — this way you will avoid unpleasant surprises at tax time.

In order to make the book-work easier, the I.R.D. have introduced a "$200 rule". If you spend less than $200 on any item it can be classified as an expense and so 100% deducted in the year of purchase. There are a few conditions to prevent abuse of this rule. Multiple billing is out. This is where you buy $1,000 worth of carpet in five $200 lots, for example. Also, where a single big job is broken down into less than $200 purchases (such as building a new $2000 carport with materials costing no more than $200 per purchase) you cannot use the $200 rule.

Examples of items of expenses are:

- Interest on loans borrowed to purchase the property (not the principal repayments though)
- Repairs and maintenance
- Rates
- Insurance

Vehicle running expenses
Telephone line rental (50% normally.)
Subscription to daily newspaper (same percentages as with phone)
Office supplies
The cost of this book (if you already are a landlord)
Bank fees (including the up-front fees charged to set up your mortgage)
Solicitors' fees for arranging the mortgage (but not for the work of conveyancing)
Membership fees of local Property Investors Association
Accountancy fees
Fees or commissions paid to agents to manage the property

In tax law, an individual cannot employ themselves to do work on flats they own. (I can't figure any advantage to doing so anyway.) However, there may be some advantages in creating employment conditions, for example where your spouse is on a lower marginal tax rate than you. You could employ your spouse and effectively syphon off some profit into an area where a lower tax rate applies. Another case is where the property is not owned by you directly but by a limited liability company and the company is your employer or is paying company tax. Advice from your accountant is required if any of these special cases apply to you.

Most expenses are paid for by writing out a cheque. Cheque butts filled out with details of why the cheque was written become the foundation of a reliable series of payment records. There are, however two other ways expenses are paid: cash payments and bank payments.

Cash payments. It is inconvenient and expensive to write out a cheque for every little expense. For example, paying for a duplicate key costing $3.50 with a cheque wastes both my time and the shopkeeper's. I pay in cash and ask for a till receipt. On the back of the receipt I write a note describing the expense, and put it in a small box when I get home. Every few months I empty this box and categorise on a sheet of paper each expense, using the same headings as I use in my main cash book (see later). I then write a out a cheque, payable to myself, for the total amount. On the cheque butt I manage to list, in small writing, the totals of each category ready for transferring to the cash book. The receipts, together with the summary on the sheet of paper, are then sealed in an envelope and put into storage. In this way I am reimbursed, the expenses cashbook continues to have each expense categorised, and the tax requirements of record keeping are complied with. I have created what is called an "audit trail".

Automatic payments. Mortgage repayments to banks are usually paid by automatic payment. All bank fees are deducted automatically. Also, in some cases, rates and insurance can be deducted by direct debit.

At the end of the year, I go to my bank and get an annual summary of my mortgage account. This documents shows all payments made, and differentiates between interest payments and capital repayments. The total of interest payments is what I need for my tax form.

Other automatic payments such as rates and insurance can be totalled up from my bank statements for the tax form. The bank charges pop up under numerous headings such as line fees, bank fees, transaction fees, interest, and cheque duty. These have to be hunted out from among the bank statements and added up.

Vehicle running

This is another important expense. You are likely to use your private car for the odd jobs to do with your rental property. The current rule is that you need to keep a diary in the car of each business trip made in the vehicle over a period of three months. After taking this "sample", you can cease using the diary and multiply up to get a year's business running. So long as you use less than 2000 km per year the year's running can be expensed at the rate of cents per kilometre as per the Public Service mileage rates. These rates are approved by the IRD and vary each year; indeed they may vary a number of times within a year. The rates can be obtained from the IRD or from an accountant. If your business doesn't change significantly, the one 3-monthly sample can be used for up to 3 years after it was taken. If you want to claim more than 2000 km you have to base it on the actual running expenses of the vehicle.

Writing up the cash-book

The task of recording expenses from the cheque butts is essentially one of putting them into categories. **Figure 3** is an example of a cash book recording expenses. Blank cashbooks are sold with different numbers of columns. Purchase one with 8 to 16 columns.

The categories needed for one rental property are outlined on the tax form IR 3R available from the IRD. These categorise are: rates, insurance, interest, repairs, agents' collection fees, maintenance, depreciation and other.

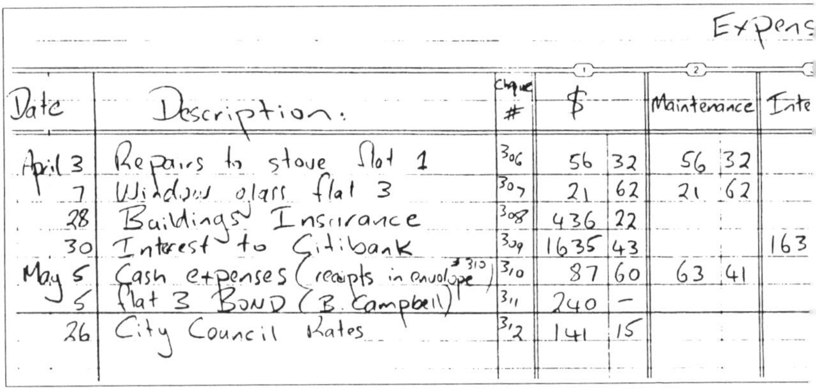

				Expens…			
Date	Description:	Cheque #	$		Maintenance		Inte…
April 3	Repairs to stove flat 1	306	56	32	56	32	
7	Window glass flat 3	307	21	62	21	62	
28	Buildings Insurance	308	436	22			
30	Interest to Citibank	309	1635	43			163
May 5	Cash expenses (receipts in envelope # 310)	310	87	60	63	41	
5	Flat 3 BOND (B. Campbell)	311	240	–			
26	City Council Rates	312	141	15			

Figure 3: Example of a cash book. (See p. 121.)

Head up your columns all these headings except perhaps agents' collection fees, which are normally irrelevant to the owner-manager. In addition, reserve the first one for the dollar amount of each cheque, another one for bond paid and a final one for capital item expenditure. I suggest another one for "advertising to-let". Thus in total a 10-column book is sufficient.

Keep the records in this book in the number order of your cheques. At the end of the year add each column to obtain the totals of each category, ready for the tax return.

Depreciation

The great thing about depreciation is that it is an expense for tax purposes, but you never have to front up with cash to pay it. Depreciation enables rental-property owners to obtain a measure of tax-free income each year. When I began buying rental property I was told that the goal of an astute investor should be to own a sufficient number of highly geared properties that in total make no taxable income, but whose depreciation allowances add up to the investor's desired tax-free annual income. Unfortunately, with low inflation and low interest rates it is not so easy (and rather more risky) to arrange your affairs this way. Normally you make a profit and end up paying tax. Furthermore there is now a depreciation claw-back tax in place, so that if the property is sold tax is then paid.

Capital items are those that are not "consumed" within the tax year, e.g. the building itself, the stove, carpets and so on. Nevertheless, these long-lasting items do devalue over time. Eventually that new carpet you

...sh Book

...dvertising to let	Rates	Insurance	Other	Bonds	Capital
		436 22			
13 05					
			12 14		
				240 —	
	141 15				

laid in flat 1 will wear out and need replacement.

There have recently been major changes to depreciation tax law, and until the tax year 1995-96 we are in transition to a new setup. There is a comprehensive free booklet (I.R. 260) available from the I.R.D. called *Depreciation: How to claim depreciation for tax purposes*. It has 88 pages, 57 of which are depreciation tables and indexes. In calculating depreciation you now have a choice of either the straight-line (S.L.) method or the diminishing-value (D.V.) method for all assets — buildings and chattels. Straight line allows for the same depreciation deduction each year, while diminishing value allow for a greater deduction in earlier years and less later. Both methods give similar results in real terms over the life of an asset. The choice of which method is best determined by individual circumstance. Seek your accountant's advice.

When calculating diminishing-value depreciation, you reduce the book value of the asset each year by the amount of deprecation claimed. Thus if you spend $1000 on carpets you claim 33% of $1000 which is $333 in the first year. This leaves a book value of $666 to start the second year with. In the second year the 33% depreciation is $220, leaving a book value of $446. On the other hand, with the straight-line method the deprecation claimed stays the same year after year. In our carpet example, the straight-line rate for carpets is 24% so $240 is deducted every year.

Whatever method you use, you need to keep track of the book value of each asset. When you come to sell the property it is almost certain that the total amount of depreciation you have claimed over the years on your buildings (and sometimes on chattels) becomes taxable income in the year of sale under the deprecation claw-back tax. For this purpose, I keep track of depreciation from one year to the next in a simple file of completed depreciation forms, to which a new form is added each year.

Depreciation on buildings

Depreciation on buildings as allowed by the I.R.D. is calculated on the value of the buildings at purchase. The value of the buildings is derived from the total cost of purchasing the property, i.e. the price you paid plus the cost of conveyancing and any other purchasing expenses you may have had. (You do not, however, include the expenses of arranging the mortgage finance — this can be fully claimed in the first year.) The total purchase expense is then divided into three portions: the value of the land, the value of the chattels, and the value of the buildings. .

You will have already made a chattels list (see p.36). If you deduct the total value of chattels from the purchase cost you are left with the value of buildings and land. As a basis for working out the buildings value you can use your valuation report that was done for the purpose of raising finance, or the government valuation. Using one of these valuations you can split the land and buildings purchase expense in the same proportions as the report does.

If you have recently purchased buildings and have owned them for less than one tax year, you claim buildings depreciation on a monthly basis. For example, if you have owned them for 5 months you claim 5/12 of a full year's depreciation.

Depreciation on chattels

Chattels are, essentially, things that are not part of the building — carpets, stove, blinds and drapes, light-fittings and so on. You may depreciate each chattel individually using either the diminishing-value or straight-line methods. Alternatively, you can pool some or all of them in order to calculate depreciation. Chattels that are being pooled must cost, or have a book value of, less than $2000 each and depreciation must be calculated by the diminishing-value method. You may put all the chattels of a block of flats in a pool, for example. The advantage of doing this is that it makes the paperwork easier. The disadvantage is that the rate used is that of the lowest in the pool. For example carpets, allowable at 33% on their own, are likely to be depreciated in the pool at the rate for the vinyl flooring of the kitchen — which is only 18%. (See rates below.)

If you have recently purchased chattels and have owned them for less than a year, you claim depreciation on a monthly basis. The higher the value of the chattels, the greater the depreciation you can claim in the first few years of their life, and so the lower will be your taxable income.

Depreciation rates

With the changes to the depreciation regime there is now something of a complex assortment of depreciation rates.

Rates for buildings depreciation

For buildings acquired before 1 April 1993: There are three categories of buildings, each with different rates. You can choose either the old straight-line rates or you can now (in two categories at least) change to some new diminishing-value rates:

- Reinforced concrete throughout, steel, or reinforced concrete framed with brick walls, or permanent materials: D.V. 1%, S.L. 1%
- Brick, stone, or concrete-walled buildings without steel, or reinforced concrete frame, stucco, steeltex or similar construction with wooden frame: D.V. 2.5%, S.L. 2%
- Wooden-framed (other than specified above). D.V. 3%, S.L. 2.5%

For buildings acquired after 31st March 1993: Things are a lot simpler. All buildings, irrespective of their construction, have a D.V. rate of 4% and a S.L. rate of 3%

Rates for chattels depreciation

Similar to the rates with buildings, there are two basic categories: Assets acquired *before* 1 April 1993, and assets acquired *after* 31 March 1993. However, with chattels, there is also a third category for *new* chattels acquired between 16 December 1991 and 1 April 1993.

The following table shows these three sets of rates as they appear on the back of the form IR 3R.

Depreciation on contents

Assets	acquired **before** 1 April 1993		acquired **new** between 16 December 1991 and 31 March 1993		acquired **after** 31 March 1993	
	DV%	SL%	DV%	SL%	DV%	SL%
Blinds, drapes and curtains	20	13.5	25	17.5	22	15.5
Carpets	20	13.5	25	17.5	33	24
Dishwashers	10	7	12.5	8.5	26	18
Furniture (loose)	20	13.5	25	17.5	18	12.5
Lawn mowers	20	13.5	25	17.5	40	30
Light fittings	10	7	12.5	8.5	18	12.5
Ovens	10	7	12.5	8.5	22	15.5
Refrigerators and freezers	10	7	12.5	8.5	22	15.5
Televisions, videos and stereos	20	13.5	25	17.5	18	12.5
Vinyl flooring	20	13.5	25	17.5	18	12.5
Washing machines and dryers	10	7	12.5	8.5	26	18

For a more detailed set of chattels the I.R.D. booklet I.R. 260 has a table of rates for assets acquired on or after 1 April 1993. This table is on the following page.

Preparing the tax form

Good record keeping throughout the year makes for an easy time at the end. For a simple one rental-property business, a summary of income and expenses as outlined above is ready for transfer onto the IR 3R, and with the addition of depreciation, the return is done. Rental-property owners do not have to use the IR 3R form (and I never have) but it seems to me a perfectly good one to use if you have only one or two properties.

Residential Rental Property Chattels

	Estimated useful life (years)	Diminishingn Value Rate (%)	Straight Line Rate (%)
Residential rental property chattels (default class)	5	33	24
Appliances (small)	4	40	30
Blinds	8	22	15.5
Carpets	5	33	24
Curtains	8	22	15.5
Dishwashers	6.66	26	18
Drapes	8	22	15.5
Dryers (clothes, domestic type)	6.66	26	18
Freezers (domestic type)	8	22	15.5
Furniture (fitted)	15.5	12	8
Furniture (loose)	10	18	12.5
Heaters (electric)	3	50	40
Heaters (gas, fitted)	8	22	15.5
Heaters (gas, portable)	5	33	24
Lawn mowers	4	40	30
Light fittings	10	18	12.5
Linen	3	50	40
Microwave ovens (domestic type)	6.66	26	18
Ovens (domestic type)	8	22	15.5
Refrigerators (domestic type)	8	22	15.5
Stereos	5	33	24
Stoves (domestic type)	8	22	15.5
Televisions	5	33	24
Vacuum cleaners (domestic type)	3	50	40
Video recorders	5	33	24
Vinyl flooring	10	18	12.5
Washing machines (domestic type)	6.66	26	18
Water heaters	12.5	15	10

When you own more than one property, each needs to be accounted for separately. In the case of that block of flats you bought last year, one set of accounts for that whole block is fine. However, a separate set of accounts needs to be kept for that old house down the road you bought 5 years ago and rent out in rough condition.

You can still use the one bank account for all your rental properties, and you can also use the one cash book. You will just use more columns, as you will need a set of columns for each property. (The more properties you have, the greater the advantage of organising their accounts on a computer — even if only on a spreadsheet.)

The basic end-of-year set of financial statements for the tax return is:

- An overhead-expense account
- An income and expenditure account for each property (showing a profit or loss for that property)
- A combined profit and loss account showing the overall profit (or perhaps a loss) of them all

Overhead-expense account. Most expenses will be for a particular property. When making payment, ensure you write on the cheque butt (or receipt in the case of a cash payment) the name of the property. The basic rule is to charge against each property all expenses identified with that property. However, some expenses are not specific to a particular property. For example, the tins of paint you bought cheap at a garage sale are sure to get used on more than one of your properties, but you are not yet sure which. Also, the costs of running the office, your telephone rental, newspaper, professional association fees, accountancy fees and so on.

In your cash book you will need a set of columns, each with a heading, for these overhead expenses, e.g. maintenance, accountant, office supplies, telephone rental. If you have a car just for your business, then all the annual costs of running this car can be brought to account, otherwise calculate the cost of the car as discussed on p.121.

At the end of the year, list the sub-headings with their amounts and divide the total overhead-expense amount by the number of rental units you own. This figure per unit then becomes an expense for each property according to the number of units in each. For example, a total of $4605.85 overheads divided by 10 units is $460.58 per unit. Thus a block of 5 flats would have an overhead charge of $2,300 as an expense.

The following is an example of an overhead-expense summary:

OVERHEADS ALL FLATS COMBINED	$
Advertising	187.30
Maintenance	435.81
Accountant	100.00
Answering machine depreciation	38.00
Professional bodies	206.50
Office supplies	$76.50
Bank charges	$283.48
Newspaper	176.60
1/2 telephone rental	348.34
Vehicle running	2378.00
Computer expenses	323.62
TOTAL	4605.85
Divided by 10 flats	460.58

An income and expenditure account for each property. See the following table, which summarises a typical rental operation. Throughout the year you will have closely tracked the rent, so these can be easily identified with each rental unit from your rent-inward cash book. The overhead expense has been calculated as described above. The expenses peculiar to each property are added in, including depreciation on buildings and chattels, and you will have either a profit or loss.

Sample income and expenditure account

23 Willow Ave (five flats)		
EXPENSES		
Rates		1543.04
Insurance		487.10
Maintenance		3090.49
Overheads (five flats)		2302.92
Depreciation		2900.00
Refinancing expenses		2626.76
Interest to lawyers Bothwell	8757.3	
Interest to Southland Building Society	1276.76	
Interest to Citibank	6681.84	
Total Interest		16715.89
TOTAL EXPENSES		29666.21
Profit		798.79
		30465.00
INCOME		
Rents		
Flat 1	5873.00	
Flat 2	5636.00	
Flat 3	5720.00	
Flat 4	6293.00	
Flat 5	7020.00	
Less rent refunds	-77.00	
TOTAL RENTS		30465.00

A combined profit and loss account. The profits and losses from each property are simply brought together and an overall profit or loss is identified. The following table shows an example for five rental properties. This overall result is what is transferred to your tax return.

Combined Rental Profit and Loss Account

Profit		**Loss**	
23 Waikuku Road	4721.45	49 Poole Street	426.99
2/50 College Street	1691.25		
23 Willow Ave (five flats)	798.79		
1/79 Wharf Road	3885.92	Overall Profit	10670.41
TOTALS	11097.41		11097.41

Chapter 8

Maintaining rental properties

House maintenance is a large topic. How much of the maintenance the rental-property owner will do and how much will be contracted out is completely up to the individual and depends on how much time and what skills you have. There are general house-maintenance people who offer a range of small repair services. They usually advertise locally in the areas they work. If you do have the time there is much to gain from learning to do many of the small tasks yourself.

For example, I recently did some work at one of my flats — it is in an old house. I had visited the flat a week before and made a list of jobs to be done. In two and a half hours, I mixed up some sand and cement mortar and repaired the open brick fireplace. I also fitted a new grate which I had brought along. I found that the fault with the electric range grill element was just a burnt-out fuse. The big tap over the bath was leaking, and on opening it up I found the seat had a groove in it and was already ground down, so I fitted a new stainless-steel seat. I also took to the top of the kitchen door with my plane and freed it from jamming (the old wooden piles are still slowly moving.) I also climbed onto the roof and traced a leak to a nail on some ridging, that had lost its head. I pulled it out and put a new nail in, with sealant around it for good measure. After cleaning up I left. Those jobs could have been done by separate visits from an electrician, a plumber, a brick layer and a carpenter — but at what cost?

Exterior painting

Acrylic paint is superior to enamel, except on wooded surfaces where doors and windows close. Wood on the outside of a house needs paint to preserve it. The parts of a wooden house that get the sun need re-painting at least twice as often as the shaded parts. Dark colours absorb heat from the sun and heat up the timber underneath so it is liable to crack. Thus light colours are much kinder to timber — and cheaper. Stucco walls only need painting occasionally (for the sake of appearances) and dark colours may be used if desired. The cost of painting a corrugated iron roof is not matched by any rust-prevention benefits that may be gained. If you paint a roof for the first time, be clear in your own mind you are doing so only for the appearance. Once painted, however, the paintwork needs to be maintained to control rusting where any old paint flakes off and traps moisture.

Interior decoration

Much improvement can be made by interior decorating a flat that is a bit run down. I think of the inside surface of my properties as a delicate skin overlying the real bricks and mortar. It is a skin that is easily damaged, and is either expensive or time-consuming to repair.

The first question is: how much do I do here? Complete redecoration of every room including ceilings, walls, trim, windows and floor, is a huge job. For example, I might decide only to paint the walls of the living room and leave the trim and ceiling because they are in good enough repair. When the walls are all newly painted, then the old trim and ceiling which looked O.K. before now looks rough and out of place, so maybe I'll paint them too. Then the kitchen looks dowdy alongside the new living room. It is about then that I give up. I have done complete redecorations and am aware of both their value and their cost. Redecoration does transform a property, but it costs either a lot of my time, or a lot of dollars to employ somebody else. The life of a rental-property owner is one of compromise.

Internal walls are made of a number of different materials. Gib-board is now universally used — for the very good reason that it is wonderful stuff. However, older properties may still have scrim over sarking — a system of thin sacking material (scrim) nailed over solid timber planks (sarking). When painting over old scrim, it needs to be treated carefully. Tighten it up and with nail or staple-gun anywhere it is coming loose. Put new wallpaper over places where the old paper has come off. The whole lot can then be painted over.

To do a complete renovation on a scrim wall, pull off the old wallpaper and scrim and nail on gib board. I really like the buildings I own where this has previously been done — but I have never actually spent the money and done it myself because it's a big job and I avoid big jobs that seem to me essentially cosmetic. Insurance companies, however, will often charge extra to insure a dwelling lined with scrim because it catches fire more easily. This is one advantage of replacing scrim with fire retardant gib-board.

When interior decorating, one of the first questions you will need to answer is whether to wallpaper or to paint, and if the choice is paint whether to use acrylic or enamel. Acrylic paint is usually cheaper. Enamel paint is the most durable and mould-resistant in the wet areas of bathroom and kitchen. In dry areas, vinyl wallpaper is more durable than paint. Hence I generally like to paint with acrylic in the bedrooms, use vinyl wallpaper in the living room and hallways and enamel paint in the kitchen and bathroom.

How long the interior decoration will last usually depends mainly on the thoroughness of preparation. One problem is how to prepare a wall that already has wallpaper on it. The choice is one of removing it or resurfacing over it. If it is sound and well stuck on it can be repainted or repapered. Nevertheless, it is better to get old wallpaper off, and certainly if it's not well attached and you intend to paint over it, it needs to come off. I spray it with hot water containing some detergent, using my garden sprayer. I let it soak and then perhaps wet it again and pull and rub it off. This system, unfortunately, is not so effective for waterproof vinyl paper.

When completely re-painting a room, first paint the ceiling so the fine spray and drips that come off the roller will harmlessly fall on unpainted surfaces. Next, paint the woodwork around the doors, windows and skirting boards — because you don't need to worry about getting paint on the walls where the two meet. Lastly, paint the walls. If the walls and trim are different colours, one of the tests of the finished work will be how neat the line is between the walls and trim (the "cutting in"). If replacing the carpet, paint first so the drops of paint that fall are no problem. Otherwise you will need some large pieces of material, or at least newspaper, to cover the floor. In winter an electric heater is a great aid to warm up a room and help the paint to dry.

The paint can be applied to the ceilings and walls with rollers and a brush to cut in around the edges. A roller can be kept overnight in a bucket of water. When using water-based paint, however, the roller will drip a lot when first used the next morning. If these drips are problematic, one way to avoid them is to clean the roller out and dry it overnight in a hot water cupboard. The easy way to do this is with a hose on the back lawn. Squirt the hose so the roller spins rapidly under the jet of water — and stand to the side! Between jobs during the day, enamel paint rollers can be wrapped up in a rag soaked in turps. Overnight they are best kept in a bucket of water. At the end of the job, throw them away or wash them out with turps then warm water and a lot of soap powder.

Painting the wet areas is a lot of work. They need cleaning and lightly sanding, then undercoating and top coating, both coats being with enamel paint. It is always best to do the windows in enamel because acrylic paint tends to jam them shut.

Aside from the cleaning, repainting a ceiling can be a relatively quick job that brings worthwhile results. Smoke-stained ceilings can often be cleaned satisfactorily by reaching up with a floor mop. However, cleaning by hand while perched on the top of a ladder gives the best result. Use a bucket of hot water with floor cleaner in it. In all the dry areas acrylic ceiling paint is cheap and effective, but in the wet area you are best to use enamel paint, especially if mould is likely to be a problem. I tackle mouldy places by cleaning them, then spraying on anti-mould chemical (sold at paint shops). Again, I usually use my garden sprayer, and allow to dry overnight.

New curtains matching or toning in with the rest of the room colours make a big difference. Some towns have a second-hand shop dealing in curtains — a great idea for rental-property owners. A feature lightshade in the living room is another good idea.

Carpets

These should be laid last, after all the painting has been done. For more on carpets, see p. 44, 45.

Plumbing

"That tap is leaking." From this common refrain you will soon learn that plumbers are expensive, or how a tap works. With a few tools you can do many of the small plumbing jobs around your rental property. Beside the usual handyperson's tools — pliers, shifting spanner and screwdrivers — you also need a pair of pipe tongs, a seat-cutting tool and a basin spanner (for removing hand-basin taps), assorted tap washers, replacement stainless-steel seats, thread tape, hemp, and a selection of serviceable second-hand taps and tap parts.

Home owners often upgrade their kitchens and bathrooms and in the process discard perfectly good taps in favour of more stylish ones. Whenever I see such taps, for example at a garage sale, I buy them if they're cheap. If possible I open them up and check out the condition of their seats first. If I cannot do this I still at least feel confident about buying any ones with a hot tap label on them as these are unlikely to be worn out — it is the high-pressure cold taps that wear first.

If a leaky tap is allowed to continue leaking it will within a few months wear a groove in the seat. Replacing the washer will not solve the problem: you will need to re-cut the seat using a tap cutting die. This is an essential tool for every do-it-yourself landlord.

Often re-cutting the seat won't work because it has already been cut down a number of times and the groove has become worn down past the seat in the body of the tap. Normally, in this situation you have to replace the whole tap. Often, if the groove hasn't gone too deep, stainless-steel seat inserts can be fitted into all but the oldest style of taps, and provide a virtually permanent seat. This is also quicker than replacing the whole tap. These inserts are usually available only from specialist plumbing supply shops.

The brass outdoor water tap with threaded hose connection is one item worth buying new. These are such good value for money I use them whenever I can, for example when making provision for automatic washing-machine taps inside the house.

The two taps that get the most use are the washhand-basin tap and the cold-water sink tap. Unfortunately the washhand-basin tap is also the worst tap in the house to have to replace. Removing the old one is the problem: you need a special spanner. Even with the holding nut removed, the tap is sometimes so stuck on with age that a broken hand-basin results when trying to remove it. I used to call in a plumber to do this job on difficult ones, and once he broke the hand-basin then charged me to buy and fit a replacement one. (I prefer to break my own, thank you!) Try an electric drill up under the basin to remove the age-hardened sealer gripping the tap.

The other tap in your rental-house you will become most familiar with is the ballcock tap. If you have a header-tank hot-water system you will have one up in there in the roof, and there is another in every toilet cistern. These taps use small round washers about half the size of a five-cent piece. Have a few on hand. If the tap itself needs replacing, it is cheap enough.

Most plumbing jobs start with turning off the toby (main tap). Know where to locate this on your property boundary. If you don't know, the local council will usually find it for you from their maps.

Leaking roofs

The most common roof in New Zealand is the sloping corrugated iron roof. A leaky roof must be fixed quickly. Detecting where the leak is the most difficult part. Mostly, but not always, where the leak occurs inside is directly below where the hole is in the roof. I like to measure with a tape measure from the leak to the edge of a window. Then when I am on the roof I can measure from that spot along the roof to find the place where the leak is. Often the leak is caused by a fault in the flashing, on one of the ridges or perhaps around a chimney. You may have to replace rusted flashings.

On older roofs, leaks are often caused by rusting where one sheet of iron overlaps another. (Newer roofs are made of long-run iron and so avoid this problem.) One rusty lap usually means most of the other laps are likely to be rusty as well. You probably should at this point decide to replace the whole roof. However, if you are like me you may decide to repair rather than replace, save the money and say, "Next year I'll replace the roof." A rusted-through lap can be fixed by cutting a short length of iron (preferably with the same size of corrugations as the roof), taking out the nails, slipping it under the top sheet and over the top of the bottom one. Then nail it all back on.

Other roof leaks can often be quickly fixed with a big squirt of a specialist roof sealant from a sealing gun.

Electrical work

Under the Electricity Act 1993, you can legally do some work on the house you *own and occupy.* However, with the house you rent out you cannot legally do much except replace light bulbs and fuses yourself. For everything else you need the services of a registered electrician.

Managing mildew

Research has shown mildew occurs in 46% of New Zealand residential premises, and in 1 out of 5 it is a major problem. It is a particular problem in the older type of house that we property investors tend to own. Modern houses, with their wall, ceiling and underfloor insulation are less prone to it.

Mildew grows on surfaces wet with the condensation from household activity. Unless allowed to escape outside, water vapour from baths and showers, cooking and even human breath stays inside and settles out as condensation — particularly on winter nights. It particularly occurs on walls and ceilings of back rooms that get no or little sun and are not otherwise heated.

The worst effect of mildew is that tenants don't like it, and may leave a badly affected property. In such cases they leave behind damaged internal surfaces — particularly wallpaper and ceilings, but also carpets, curtains and walls (especially walls painted with water-base paint). In winter, windows may be permanently wet with moisture running down the inside, so wooden window frames may rot along their bottom edges.

The most frustrating thing about mildew is that prevention is almost entirely up to the occupants of a house. Modern lifestyles also increase the tendency for mildew to develop. For example, houses often are shut tight day and night for security; also there are more empty houses during the day as more women as well as men are out working. Furthermore, most washing is done by having a shower instead of a bath, and clothes-drying machines are in common use.

To manage mildew, inspect your premises at the beginning of each winter. If you see any signs of mildew, discuss ways of controlling it with your tenant. For example, internal moisture can be reduced by showering with a bathroom window open and the door shut. You might instal an exit fan in the bathroom, wired to the light switch. See if you can encourage your tenants not to boil water on the stove, and to cook with a window open or an exit fan going. In the bedrooms (where the moisture is most likely to condense) advise your tenants to wipe affected surfaces with a cloth dipped in one part household beach to 4 parts water and wrung out. This not only removes the mould but also kills the spores. The bottom sill of windows can be mopped dry each morning. Opening the bedroom windows during the day will help, as will an electric heater at night on occasion. A night-store heater will often solve mildew problems. Wardrobes can grow mould. A 100-watt electric light bulb left on inside can warm it up sufficiently to prevent this, but be sure to instal it so it cannot come in direct contact with the clothes. Occupants should be discouraged from hanging wet clothes inside to dry. Clothes dryers need to be vented to the outside. Instal security catches on windows that prevent them opening more than a few centimetres, so the tenants can leave them open when they are out.

When painting or wallpapering a mildew-affected area it is important to do a good job of killing the fungus. Just wiping it away is not enough as it will have penetrated into the fabric of the wall or ceiling and simply grow back even though it is under paint or wallpaper. You need to apply a fungicide recommended by a paint retailer to kill it.

Glossary

Adjudicator: The "judge" of the local tenancy tribunal.

Assignment: When a tenant signs over their rights and responsibilities of a tenancy to another tenant. Needs the written approval of the landlord.

Automatic payment: The transfer of money from one bank account to another on a regular basis. Often used by tenant to pay rent.

Bond: A sum of money paid by a tenant at the start of a tenancy. Its purpose is be available to the landlord should the tenant default in any of their obligations. Under NZ law the bond must be held by Tenancy Services.

Business test: The test applied by Inland Revenue to differentiate between businesses (which have the intention and reasonable prospect of making a profit) and non-profit making activities such as hobbies and charities.

Capital gain: The increase in the value of property over time. Conversely, when value decreases there is incurred a capital loss.

Capitalisation rate: (Also known as rate of return.) The gross capitalisation rate is calculated by taking the income of an asset and dividing it by the value of that asset and expressing the result as a percentage. The net capitalisation rate is calculated when regular expenses, except those of borrowed funds, are first deducted from the income.

Chattels: Things in or on a building that are not a structural part of the building. For example, T.V. aerials, carpets, light fittings.

Deposit: As used in this book, the total amount of money an owner contributes towards the purchase of a property — the balance of the purchase price is made up of borrowed money.

Depreciation: The gradual reduction in value of an asset over time, through normal wear and obsolescence. The I.R.D. publishes depreciation rates which may be used to calculate an annual depreciation expense for taxation purposes.

Equity: The value of an asset or a group of assets minus the owner's borrowing. Similar to deposit except that, unlike deposit, equity changes over time as values and borrowing change.

Exemplary damages: When the Tenancy Tribunal orders a sum of money to be paid by one party to the other party as punishment for a breach of the Tenancy Act.

Expenses: Money that the I.R.D. allow you to deduct from the total rents received when calculating taxable income in any one year.

Fixed-term tenancy: A tenancy agreement that at the time it is entered into has a defined end date.

Gross rate of return: Same as gross capitalisation rate.

Letting agent: A business person who arranges for tenants and landlords to meet, but unlike a property manager, does not collect rent or manage property.

Maintenance expenses: Tax-deductable expenditure incurred in maintenance and repair of property.

Mediator: A person appointed by Tenancy Services to convene a meeting of a tenant and a landlord in dispute. The mediator's job is to help the two parties to come to a settlement, but he/she has no power to impose one (if one is needed the adjudicator does it).

Mortgage: The pledging of real estate as security for a debt. Often used to refer to the amount of the debt.

Mortgagee: The "person" (usually a bank) who lends money on a mortgage.
Mortgagor: The borrower.
Negative gearing: When the expenses of a property are greater than the income from it.
Net worth. A measure of wealth. Everything an individual owns less all debts is net worth.
Notices: The passing of written information (subject to a particular provision in the Tenancy Act) between landlords and tenants, or vice-versa.
Option to rent: A contract whereby a prospective tenant pays a sum of money to a landlord who in return, for an agreed period of time, gives them an unfettered right to take up the tenancy.
Overhead expense: A property expense that cannot be identified with one particular property. It is spread across all properties owned.
Paid-to date: The date a tenant has currently paid the rent to.
Partnership: Where two or more tenants enter into and sign the same tenancy agreement. (There may also be a partnership of landlords.)
Periodic tenancy: A tenancy that can be terminated by either the landlord or tenant subject to those periods of notice as specified in the Tenancy Act. (Periodic tenancies are the most common type of tenancy.)
Rate of return: *See* **Capitalisation rate.**
Spreadsheet: A computer program designed for recording and manipulating data (including financial data). In operation and appearance on the screen, spreadsheets resemble a huge sheet of paper with a matrix of horizontal and vertical lines.
Sublet: When a tenant enters into a tenancy agreement with another tenant for all or part of the premises they themselves rent. Subletting differs from assignment in that the initial relationship between the first tenant and landlord remains in place. Subletting needs the written approval of the landlord. Subletting is common in commercial property but not in residential.
Tainting: An informal term used in taxation. Describes the process whereby one type of business activity of a tax payer has an unplanned and negative taxation effect upon another. For example, an owner of rental property also engaging in property development in such a way that all of his/her property transactions become assessed as development (and so he/she becomes subject to income tax on all property value rises at the time of sale.)
Tax deductibility: The ability to set an expense off against income and thus reduce net income for tax purposes.
Ten-day letter. A notice given under s. 56(b)(i) of the Tenancy Act by either a tenant or a landlord to the other party. It gives 10 working days to remedy a breach of the act or tenancy agreement. Commonly given by landlords to tenants who are in arrears of rent.
Tenancy agreement: The relationship between a landlord and the occupier of a property. The law requires it to be written (although unwritten ones still have the force of tenancy law).
Tenancy at large: A term describing the situation where a tenant pays a landlord rent money but has not verbally or otherwise defined any other details of a tenancy agreement with the landlord.
Tenancy Services: A division of the Ministry of Housing charged with administering the Tenancy Act up to the point of the tenancy tribunal. (The tribunal is administered by the Department of Justice.)

Appendix 1

List of useful contacts in the business

New Zealand Property Investors Federation. P.O. Box 4396 Christchurch Ph. (03) 366-5978. There are also a number of local property investors associations throughout New Zealand. To locate your local association, ask the Property Investors Federation or a real estate agent, or inquire through your local Citizens' Advice Bureau.

Bay Collection Agency. Toll-free number 0800 800 790. Private Bag 92505, Wellesley Street, Auckland.

Bond Processing Centre. P.O. Box 50445, Porirua. Toll-free number 0800 737 666. Phone (04) 237-0246. Fax (04) 237-7884

Estate Magazine. P.O. Box 22-793, Christchurch.

On the House (a first-rate landlord's newsletter) P.O. Box 470 Dunedin Ph/Fax 03 453-0066

After-hours landlord advice. Ph 0900-55400 (calls cost $4.00 a minute)

G.P. Legislation (where you buy the Tenancy Act) (04) 496 5655

"Enforcing your Judgment or Money Order" A $37.00 A4 size workbook published by the author Scotney Williams LLB., 4 Portland Rd, Remuera, Auckland Ph (09) 524 6679.

Tenancy Services offices

Whangarei
Link Centre
1 Robert St
Laurie Hall Park
P.O. Box 1755
Whangarei
Ph 09 438 6980
Fax 09 438 5210

Takapuna
GRE House
12/14 Northcroft St
P.O. Box 331 431
Takapuna
Ph 09 489 4155
Fax 09 486 0929

Auckland
Level 11
Reserve Bank Building
Cnr Customs and Gore Streets
P.O. Box 2220
Auckland
Ph 09 357 5450
Fax 09 302 0253

Henderson
Lincoln Manor
295 Lincoln Rd
P.O. Box 104 081
Henderson
Ph 09 836 3124
Fax 09 838 9850

Manukau
Level 1
Westpac Building
627 Great South Road
P.O. Box 76 451
Manukau
Ph 09 262 4329
Fax 09 263 6013

Hamilton
WEL Energy Trust Building
Cnr Bryce & Victoria St
Private Bag 3124
Hamilton
Ph 07 834 1569
Fax 07 834 1571

Tauranga
195 Devonport Road
P.O. Box 13 108
Tauranga
Ph 07 578 4167
Fax 07 578 8429

Rotorua
40 Pukaki St
P.O. Box 630
Rotorua
Ph 07 349 0020
Fax 07 348 0482

Gisborne
Quaypoint Building
Gladstone Rd
P.O. Box 254
Gisborne
Ph 06 868 1461
Fax 06 868 1964

Napier
Somerset Smith House
Civic Court
1st Floor
Station Street
P.O. Box 349
Napier
Ph 06 834 0732
Fax 06 834 4667

New Plymouth
11 Robe St
Ground Floor
P.O. Box 331
New Plymouth
Ph 06 759 8016
Fax 06 759 8094

Palmerston North
4th Floor, State Insurance Building
61-75 Rangitikei St
P.O. Box 1895
Palmerston North
Ph 06 355 4026
Fax 06 355 4029

Lower Hutt
Level 1
46-50 Bloomfield Tce
P.O. Box 30 400
Lower Hutt
Ph 04 570 6111
Fax 04 570 6115

Wellington
Level 11, Vogel Building
Aitken St
P.O. Box 10 797
Wellington
Ph 04 471 6900
Fax 04 472 8828

Blenheim
141 High Street
P.O. Box 309
Blenheim
Ph 03 578 1958
Fax 03 577 9966

Nelson
9 Buxton Square
P.O. Box 1149
Nelson
Ph 03 548 3957
Fax 03 548 2488

Greymouth
109 Mackey Street
P.O. Box 33
Greymouth
Ph 03 768 4190
Fax 03 768 4200

Christchurch
5th Floor, 159 Manchester St
P.O. Box 22 725
Christchurch
Ph 03 371 2100
Fax 03 379 8324

Timaru
Ballantyne's Building
7 Canon St
P.O. Box 388
Timaru
Ph & Fax 03 684 9481

Dunedin
3rd Floor, Capitol Building
67 Princess St
Moray Place
P.O. Box 5778
Dunedin
Ph 03 479 3880
Fax 03 477 8884

Invercargill
55-59 Gala St
Private Bag 90 118
Invercargill
Ph 03 214 1720
Fax 03 218 2426

Appendix 2: Rental application form

RENTAL APPLICATION

for the property at..

Name:..

Date of Birth........................Home phone...............................Work phone..........................

A PERSONAL IDENTIFICATION NUMBER..
(Credit card Number, I.S.S. Number, Driver's License Number, etc. Please state)

PRESENT ADDRESS...

How long at this address?.......................................Rent $............................Bond $....................

Reason for moving?...

Landlord/Manager of this address..Phone.........................

Any Pets? yes / no (circle one) If Yes, describe:...

Name and relationship of other persons to live in the dwelling ....

....

....

PRESENT OCCUPATION (or source of income):..

Employer's Name...Phone...............................

How long with this employer?...

Current gross income $............................. Per week/fortnight (circle one)

Can you obtain references? YES \ NO What Type? WORK\LANDLORD

Name of a person giving a reference....................................Phone Number.....................

VEHICLE
Make ....Year........................Number plate...................................

I declare that the statements above are true and correct, and I hereby authorize verification of references given and a credit check.

Date:.....................................Signed..

This form reproduced with permission from *Landlording in New Zealand* by Frank Saxton, available from Box 790, Nelson

Appendix 3: Offer of tenancy form

To:... From..

....

....(name and address of tenant) .... (name and address of andlord)

DATE:..

OFFER OF TENANCY ON: ....

(NOTE : This is **not** a Tenancy Agreement)

I **offer** you the Tenancy of this furnished / unfurnished house / flat on the following conditions:

1. Tenancy to begin on.. (date)
2. Rent $......................... per week / fortnight (delete one).
3. Bond $.........................
4. Signing of Tenancy Agreement, with the following conditions:-

   i.) First part-period rent of $................... due on.............................. (date)

   ii.) First regular rent of $................... due on.............................. (date)

   iii.)..

   iv.)..

Acceptance of this offer can only be by:

1. Payment of Bond $......................... and first rent of $....................... **TOTAL $**............................

and,

2. Signing of Tenancy Agreement.

This offer expires at.............................(time) on...(date).

Yours faithfully,

Signed...

Landlord / Landlord's Agent.

This form reproduced with permission from *Landlording in New Zealand* by Frank Saxton, available from Box 790, Nelson

Appendix 4: Option for tenancy

To.. From..

....

....(name and address of applicant) ....(name and address of landlord)

OPTION FOR TENANCY

Address of premises:..

Option price (maximum one week's rent): $..

Option period ends Date:.......................Time:..................................

In consideration of the option price the landlord agrees to allow the applicant an option period beginning from the date of the signing of this form and ending at the "option period ends" date and time above (time being of the essence). During this option period the landlord cannot enter into a tenancy agreement for the premises above with any person other than the applicant. The applicant may at any time during the option period enter into a tenancy agreement with the landlord under the following conditions:

1. Tenancy to begin on...
2. Rent $......................per week/fortnight (delete one)
3. Bond $...................
4. Signing of tenancy agreement, with the following conditions:

   i. First part-period rent of $.........................due on..

   ii...

   iii..

Acceptance of this option can only be by:

1. Payment of: Bond $.................

   first rent of $.................

   Sub-total $.................

   Minus option price $.................

   TOTAL $................. and,

2. Signing of Tenancy Agreement.

   Note:
   (a). In the event of the applicant not exercising the option to enter into a tenancy agreement, the landlord may retain the sum paid for this option.

   (b). This is **not** a Tenancy Agreement.

Signed.. Date...
Signature of Landlord / Landlord's Agent

This form reproduced with permission from *Landlording in New Zealand* by Frank Saxton, available from Box 790, Nelson

Appendix 5: Guarantee

GUARANTEE

LANDLORD..

TENANT...

TENANCY: Address...start date:..................................

1. The Guarantor named below hereby guarantees the due and punctual payment to the Landlord by the Tenant of all rent and other moneys payable by the Tenant under the attached Tenancy Agreement AND the observance by the tenant of all their responsibilities contained in the Tenancy Agreement and also as specified under the Residential Tenancies Act 1986.

2. The Guarantor named below hereby agrees that no indulgence, granting of time, of forbearance to sue by the Landlord or any other thing whereby the Guarantor would be released as a surety will in any way release the Guarantor from any liability hereunder.

3. The Guarantor named below hereby agrees to accept the jurisdiction of the Disputes Tribunal and the District Court in any dispute between the Landlord and the Guarantor arising out of the Tenancy Agreement and this Guarantee .

Dated this.......................................day of...19.........

Signed...*(Guarantor)*

Full name of Guarantor..

Address for service of Guarantor..
(address where all documents are to be sent)

Phone number..

Signed by the above named Guarantor in the presence of:

Witness..
(signature)

Full name of Witness...

Occupation of Witness...

Address of Witness...

This form reproduced with permission from *Landlording in New Zealand* by Frank Saxton, available from Box 790, Nelson

Appendix 6: Notice of entry

To:.. From...

....

....(name and address of tenant) ....(name and address of landlord)

Date...

NOTICE OF INTENTION TO ENTER PREMISES

As Tenant of the premises at ....

Under Section 48 of the Residential Tenancies Act 1986 please take notice that I intend to enter the above premises.

at.............................(time) on ....(date) for the purposes of:

(Delete as required)
(a) an inspection.

(b) to carry out repairs/maintenance to...

....

(c) to see if required work (namely)..

....
has been carried out.

(d) to show the premises to prospective purchasers/tenants

Signed..
Landlord / Landlord's Agent

This form reproduced with permission from *Landlording in New Zealand* by Frank Saxton, available from Box 790, Nelson

Appendix 7: Notice to terminate tenancy

To:.. From...

....

....(name and address of tenant) ....(name and address of landlord)

Date..

LANDLORD'S NOTICE TO TERMINATE TENANCY

As Tenant of the premises at ....

Under the provisions of Section 51 of the Residential Tenancies Act 1986 I give you notice your tenancy will terminate on...(date).

My reason for giving you less than 90 days notice is:

....

....

....

....

....

....

....

Signed..
Landlord / Landlord's Agent

This form reproduced with permission from *Landlording in New Zealand* by Frank Saxton, available from Box 790, Nelson

Appendix 8: 10 day notice to remedy

To.. From...

....

....(name and address of tenant) ....(name and address of landlord)

Date..

10 DAY NOTICE TO REMEDY

PURSUANT TO SECTION 56 OF THE RESIDENTIAL TENANCIES ACT 1986.

As Tenant of the premises at ....

I,..being the Landlord/Landlord's agent hereby give you 10 working days' notice to remedy the breach of the tenancy agreement/provisions of the act *(delete one)*, as set out below:

....

....

....

....

....

....

....

....

....

TAKE NOTICE THAT IF YOU FAIL OR REFUSE to remedy the breach within the time specified, the landlord will be entitled to apply to the Tenancy Tribunal for an order to:
1. remedy the breach.
2. request compensation
3. **terminate the tenancy**

Signed..

Landlord / Landlord's Agent

This form reproduced with permission from *Landlording in New Zealand* by Frank Saxton, available from Box 790, Nelson

Appendix 9: Notice of rent increase

TO:... FROM: ....

....

.... (name and address of tenant) .... (name and address of landlord)

DATE:..

NOTICE OF INCREASE IN RENT

As Tenant of the premises at...

I hereby give you at least 60 days notice (under Section 24 of the Residential Tenancies Act 1986)

that your rent will be increased to $......................... per.......................... To take effect

on and from the rent due date of...

Yours faithfully,

Signed..

Landlord / Landlord's Agent.

This form reproduced with permission from *Landlording in New Zealand* by Frank Saxton, available from Box 790, Nelson

Appendix 10: Notice of sale

TO:.. FROM: ....

....

.... (name and address of tenant) .... (name and address of landlord)

DATE:..

LANDLORD'S NOTICE THAT PROPERTY IS FOR SALE.

As Tenant of the premises at..

I hereby give you notice (under Section 47 of the Residential Tenancies Act 1986) that this property has been advertised for sale.

Yours faithfully,

Signed..
Landlord / Landlord's Agent.

This form reproduced with permission from *Landlording in New Zealand* by Frank Saxton, available from Box 790, Nelson

Index